Computer Systems Architecture

Also from Lexden Publishing:

Computer Systems Architecture

Robert M Newman, BSc, PhD
Elena Gaura, BSc, MSc, PhD
Dominic Hibbs, BSc, BA

Computing series editor:
Peter Hodson

Lexden Publishing Ltd

Published by Lexden Publishing Ltd in 2005
First published in 2003 by Learning Matters Ltd.

British Library Cataloguing in Publication Data
A CIP record for this book is available from the British Library.

ISBN-10: 1-904995-09-8
ISBN-13: 978-1-904995-09-8
Previous ISBN: 1-903337-07-0

Text design by Code 5 Design
Typeset by PDQ Typesetting, Newcastle under Lyme

Printed and bound by Lightning Source

Lexden Publishing Ltd
Email: info@lexden-publishing.co.uk
www.lexden-publishing.co.uk

Contents

Introduction
Studying computer
systems at degree level

Which courses this book covers

This study guide is designed for students studying introductory computer architecture courses as part of a Computer Science related degree. Different institutions take a different view of what range of 'hardware' or 'architectural' issues should be covered in the first year of a degree course, but most of them still find it a topic area important enough to warrant all Computer Science and Information Technology students studying it. These courses and modules have a variety of titles including 'Computer Architecture', 'Computer Systems', 'Computer Platforms' or 'Computing Machines', among others, often in combination with the words 'Introduction to' or the suffix 'I'. If you are studying a course, unit or module with such a title, then it is likely that there will be a fair overlap with the contents of this book.

As for the contents, the starting point for the syllabus covered in this book is the Edexcel BTEC Higher National Diploma Unit 1, Computer Platforms. However, as a degree level book this aims more towards understanding of the underlying principles behind the study rather than demonstration of practical skills (which are important too, but less likely to be a component of Degree level study). This seems to be a good basis for coverage of most of the syllabuses for similar modules we have seen, and hopefully will ensure that most of the topics in such courses will be discussed here.

In the context of this book an 'architecture' or 'platform' means the computational infrastructure necessary to support the running of a modern application program. For that reason we include software components of the architecture such as operating systems and windowed user interface, and our view of an 'application' is that it is as likely to be a fully interactive, graphics based program as a batch mode data processing program.

We have also taken the point of view that networking is an integral part of the modern computer system. For this reason, the book includes two chapters on the basic concepts of network systems.

Learning outcomes

The Quality Assurance Agency for Higher Education in England and Wales (the QAA) has been promulgating a quiet revolution in practice in universities, the framing of the objectives of all courses in 'learning outcomes'. This book is aligned with this practice, so throughout the book sections are introduced in terms of (intended) learning outcomes, the skills and knowledge that you should be able to acquire as a result of the study in the book. Overall, the book itself should have learning outcomes too. Here they are:

- To be able to use the basic descriptive and design methods of digital computer hardware, namely Boolean algebra and gate level logic diagrams to describe the operation of the subsystems of a Von Neumann computer at the lowest level.

- To be able to describe the basic hardware subsystems of a computer, including the processor, memory hierarchy, peripheral subsystems and the means used to interconnect them.
- To be able to describe the impact of the specification of different parts of a computer on its performance in different applications, and to use that knowledge to make a qualitative analysis of performance issues and plan system upgrades appropriately.
- To be able to discuss the function of an operating system in providing a programming interface and user interface for applications programs, be able to describe the subsystems of a modern operating system and be able to produce simple examples of the use of a given applications programming interface.
- To be able to discuss the basic concepts of networking, based around the conceptual framework of the ISO OSI seven layer model, and be able to relate the functioning of some common local area network systems, and describe in overview how larger networks, up to and including the Internet, are built by interconnecting such networks, and describe the protocols and addressing mechanisms on which these depend.

Your course is likely to be defined in terms of learning outcomes too. Every university produces its own, so yours are unlikely be exactly the same as above, but if they seem to be on the same lines, this book can probably help you.

Using learning outcomes to plan your study

Learning outcomes are supposed to be directly assessed. This means that practical outcomes will be assessed by practical work, or coursework. More theoretical ones will be assessed by assignments, tests and examinations. You have to show capability in all of the learning outcomes, so don't miss an assessment – very often missing one means you risk failing everything, even though it might be a small part of the mark.

This subject area used to be very practically based, building logic circuits on breadboards. This tends to be less the case now, since it's not relevant to the way modern computers are constructed, so there is less of this type of practical work. Sometimes it has been replaced by work on logic simulators such as 'crocodile clips'. If this is the case where you're studying, it's worthwhile putting in plenty of practice with the package concerned before any assessment.

Otherwise, 'practical' assessment is likely to be paper based, maybe based on small design assignments, analytical essays or, increasingly commonly, phased tests, conducted on or off line. The multiple-choice questions throughout this book will help you prepare for these. Where there is a chance to undertake an extended exercise to test more advanced skills we have included suitable exercises as well.

What's in the book

The main role of computer architecture courses in the first year of a computer science degree is to provide you with the basic underpinning needed to understand what's going on inside the computers, and therefore a lot of the background knowledge which other parts of the degree course take for granted. Mostly this is hardware, but a modern 'computer platform' is a software/hardware hybrid, so we have included both in this book.

Your understanding also needs to be up to date, and a modern desktop computer includes facilities that could only be found in multi-million dollar supercomputers just ten years ago. While a full understanding of all of these topics is undoubtedly beyond the scope of this book, to have a knowledge of how the computer in front of you works means knowing, at least in outline, these topics, and we introduce them here.

Networking is sufficiently important as a topic in modern computing to merit two dedicated chapters at the end of the book. These are broadly based on the content of the first semester of the CISCO CNAA courses, which is a component of many such courses.

Textbooks

You'll probably be recommended a textbook, but here are a few suggestions if you want something that goes into more detail than this book.

Bartee, Thomas C. (1991) *Computer Architecture and Logic Design*, McGraw-Hill, London. ISBN 0-07-003909-7.
Mano, M. Morris (1993) *Computer System Architecture*, Prentice-Hall, New Jersey USA. ISBN 0-13-175738-5.
Mano, M. Morris and Kime, Charles R. (1997) *Logic Computer Design Fundamentals*, Prentice-Hall, New Jersey USA. ISBN 0-13-182098-2.
Protopapas, D. A. (1998) *Microcomputer Hardware Design*, Prentice-Hall, New Jersey USA. ISBN 0-13-582115-0.

Chapter 1
What is a computer?

Chapter summary

The purpose of this first chapter is to set the stage for the chapters that follow by giving you a sense of what computers do, present a brief history of computers and introduce the main components of a general-purpose computer and the way these components interact to process data.

Learning outcomes

After studying this chapter you should aim to check your knowledge against the outcomes below and test your achievement by answering the multiple-choice questions at the end of the chapter. You should be able to:

Outcome 1: Explain the meaning of the terms 'data' and 'information'.
Outcome 2: Be aware of the evolution of computing technology and be able to elaborate on the future of computers.
Outcome 3: List the components of a computer system.
Outcome 4: Explain the concept of 'stored program'.
Outcome 5: Explain the role of CPU, input and output systems and memory, within a modern computer system.

How will you be assessed on this?

If you are assessed directly on it at all, it is likely to be on the basis of your understanding of definitions and facts.

Useful information sources

The Computer Language Co. Inc., (1998) *Computer Desktop Encyclopedia*, http://www.ComputerEncyclopedia.Com/

Section 1

Data, information and the 'stored program' concept

This section starts by clarifying the concepts of data and information in the context of computers and introduces the concept of 'stored program'.

CRUCIAL CONCEPTS

Tyche Brahe, the medieval astronomer, spent his adult life observing and recording the position of the planets. His successor, Johannes Kepler, analysed those records to produce laws of planetary motion. Brahe collected **data**, Kepler's Laws are **information**.

Processing data extracts its meaning. A computer is a data processing machine. Data flows into the machine as input. Information flows from the machine as output.

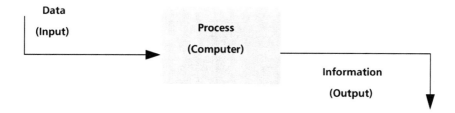

What makes a computer different from a calculator, given that they are both able to compute? To add two numbers on a calculator you:

- enter the first number;
- press the add (+) button;
- enter the second number;
- press the result (=) button;
- record the number for future reference.

The calculator finds the sum but you provide control by deciding which button to push next. A computer processes data *automatically*. It must be given a set of instructions called a program to guide it. The program is stored inside the machine and is therefore called a stored program.

CRUCIAL CONCEPT

A **computer** is a machine that processes data into information under the control of a stored program.

Historical development of computers

To fully understand and appreciate the impact computers have on our lives, and promises they hold for the future, it is important to understand their evolution.

Before computers – early computing machines and inventors
Some precursors to computers:

- The abacus emerged about 5000 years ago in Asia.
- Navigational tables started to be used in the 1600s.
- Logarithms and a primitive slide rule in use by 1617.
- Adding machine built by Blaise Pascal in 1642.

In the 1800s the industrial revolution brought both an increased need for data processing and rapidly evolving technology.

In 1822 Charles Babbage (1791–1871) proposed a steam-powered machine to perform differential equations. Ten years later he began work on the first general-purpose computer, called the Analytical Engine. The machine had a stored program, it outlined the basic elements of a modern computer and was a breakthrough concept.

In 1889, the American inventor Herman Hollerith built a machine which compiled results mechanically, accessing data stored on perforated cards. Hollerith's company later became International Business Machines (IBM, 1924).

First generation computers (1945-1956)
In the late 1940s the British COLOSSUS and the American ENIAC appeared. Neither could store their own program and needed constant manual intervention. In 1945 John von Neumann designed the Electronic Discrete Variable Automatic Computer (EDVAC) with a

memory to hold a 'stored program' as well as data and a central processing unit, which allowed all computer functions to be coordinated through a single source.

The first 'stored program' machine was built in 1948, at Manchester University. The 1950s saw computers being built both in the UK and the USA.

First generation computers used electronic tubes and magnetic drums for data storage and were massive in size and power consumption. They required an army of operators and programmers to function. Each computer had a different 'machine language' that told it how to operate.

Second generation computers (1956–1963)
In second generation computers transistors replaced tubes. Coupled with advances in magnetic-core memory, transistors led to computers that were smaller, faster, more reliable and more energy-efficient than their predecessors. Early supercomputers, able to handle enormous amounts of data, were built by IBM. Machine language was replaced by assembly language, allowing easier programming.

Second generation computers contained all the components associated with the modern day computer: printer, tape storage, disk storage, memory, operating systems and stored programs. Two high level languages, COBOL (COmmon Business Oriented Language) and FORTRAN (FORmula TRANslation) came into common use. New types of careers (programmer, analyst and computer system expert) and the entire software industry began with the second-generation computers.

Third generation computers (1964–1971)
In 1958 the 'integrated circuit' combined several electronic components on a small silicon 'chip', paving the way for third generation computers. 'Operating systems' allowed machines to run many different programs at once, with a central program that monitored and coordinated the computer's resources.

Fourth generation computers (1971–present)
The central processing unit was now a single chip – a 'microprocessor'. By 1975 the first personal computers were sold to hobbyists. In 1981 IBM sold the first PC. The number of computers in use increased from 2 million in 1981 to 5.5 million in 1982, to reach 65 million ten years later. They continued their trend towards a smaller size, working their way from desktop, to laptop computers, to palmtop. Year on year speed increased and price fell.

Computers became more widespread in the workplace, they could be linked together, or networked, to share memory space, software and information and to communicate with each other. As opposed to a mainframe computer, which was one powerful computer that shared time with many terminals for many applications, networked computers allowed individual computers to form electronic co-ops. Using direct wiring, called local area network (LAN), or telephone lines, these networks could reach enormous proportions. A global web of computer circuitry, the Internet for example, links computers worldwide into a single network of information.

Fifth generation computers (present and beyond)
The fifth generation of computers is still being developed. Some of the qualitative differences from the fourth generation might include various aspects of 'artificial intelligence', computers which can:

- use natural language;
- apply deductive reasoning;
- 'learn' from experience;

- 'see' and recognise objects;
- 'evolve' to meet new requirements.

The enablers for these capabilities may be parallel processing, which harnesses many processors together to provide enormous data throughput, and new processing technologies including superconductivity, which allow the passage of electrical signals without resistance, providing much faster processing and lower power.

Section 2

The basic subsystems of a computer

This section discusses the basic subsystems of a computer, showing in brief how the components are connected, what their functions are, and how they are tied together to form a PC.

System components: basic components

The computer system consists of a central unit (sometimes referred to as the computer) and various peripherals. The central unit, which contains most of the working electronics, is connected with cables to the peripherals.

Von Neumann broke the computer hardware down into five primary parts:

- CPU
- Input
- Output
- Working memory
- Permanent memory.

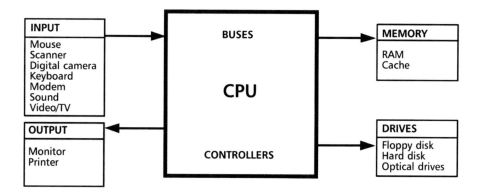

CRUCIAL CONCEPT

The **Central Processing Unit** (CPU) is the most important computer system component. Under the control of the stored programs, this unit manipulates the data and stores the results back in memory.

The CPU continually receives instructions to be executed. Each instruction is a data processing order. The work itself consists mostly of calculations and data transport. The data come from the RAM and the peripheral devices (keyboard, drives, etc). After processing, the data is sent back to RAM and the peripherals.

Memory and drives

The main memory of the computer stores the data and holds the programs. All the data which the PC uses and works with during processing are stored here. When the CPU works with data which is stored on drives (typically the hard drive), that data must be read into the working memory.

Associated with the computer system there are alternative data storage-type memories, called secondary storage or drives. Examples include CD-ROM, floppy disks and tapes.

Peripheral devices

Typically, over 80% of the cost of a computer system is due to peripheral devices.

CRUCIAL CONCEPT

A **peripheral device** is on the periphery of the computer – as distinct from the central processor and main memory, which form the heart of the computer.

The number and types of peripheral devices depend on the main application for which the computer system is intended. A small personal computer may only have a few devices such as keyboard, monitor, disk storage and a printer. A large commercial system may have many devices attached and many instances of one device. Generally, peripheral devices are classified into:

- Input devices – provide data input facilities (e.g. keyboard).
- Output devices – provide the user with the processed data/information (e.g. monitor, printer).

With the view of the above description, a computer system can be described as follows.

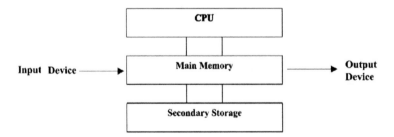

The buses

The buses are 'the nerve system' of the computer, which connect the central processing unit to all the other components. The computer system receives and sends its data from and to buses. They can be divided into:

- the system bus, which connects the CPU with RAM;
- the I/O buses, which connect the CPU with other components.

The system bus is the central bus. The I/O buses move data. They connect all I/O devices with the CPU and RAM.

CRUCIAL CONCEPT

The **input process output cycle** is the basic sequence of operations that a computer uses to process data.

An example of the steps to be performed for a computer to fulfil a task is given below.

1. Store a program in memory (given the program, the CPU can begin processing data).

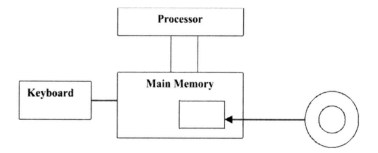

2. Input data from the keyboard is stored in memory.

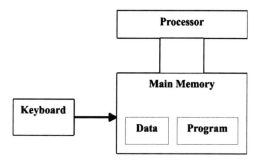

3. The processor manipulates the data and stores the results back in memory.

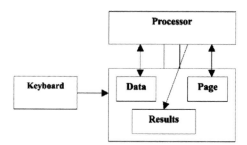

4. Results are delivered by the output device chosen (display/printer).

CRUCIAL CONCEPTS

The computer's physical components are called its **hardware** (CPU, Memory, I/O Devices). Programs and data, on the other hand, only exist as electronic pulses found in memory, and are called **software**. A series of instructions that performs a particular task is called a **program**. The American spelling (ending in –m) is always used in the context of computing.

The two major categories of software are system software and application software. System software is made up of control programs such as the operating system and database management system (DBMS).

A common misconception is that software is data. Software tells the hardware how to process the data. Software is 'run.' Data is 'processed.'

─── CRUCIAL CONCEPTS ───

System software is programs used to control the computer and develop and run application programs. It includes operating systems, network operating systems and database managers. **Applications software** is any data entry, update, query, report or other program that processes data for the user. Applications software includes the generic productivity software (spreadsheets, word processors, database programs, etc) as well as custom and packaged programs for payroll, billing, inventory and other purposes.

Hardware

The term 'hardware' means machinery and equipment (CPU, disks, tapes, etc). Hardware is concerned with storage and transmission. The more memory and disk storage a computer has, the more work it can do. The faster the memory and disks transmit data and instructions to the CPU, the faster the work gets done.

Studying computer systems architectures

The above is a general view of the structure of a computer system and how it operates. Now we can start looking at each major component in detail.

The diagram shows how different levels of study build on those below. We are going to start by looking at the logic elements which form the basic building blocks of the computer system hardware and combine them to obtain a simple computing machine. This will be followed by some information on operating systems. The last two higher levels of study of the computer system do not form the object of this book.

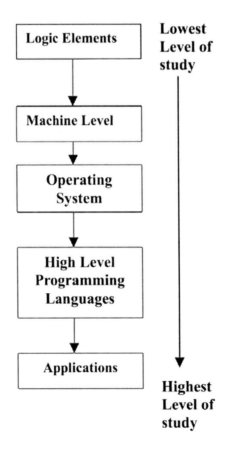

Section 3

End of chapter assessment

Multiple choice questions

1. A computer processes data:
    a) under direct human control
    b) under the control of a stored program
    c) randomly
    d) using its own intelligence
    e) none of the above

2. What distinguishes a computer from other types of calculating devices?
    a) the high number of keys
    b) the existence of a monitor
    c) the stored program
    d) the type of information
    e) Windows

3. Second generation computers were made possible by:
    a) the invention of the transistor
    b) the development of the microprocessor
    c) the development of integrated circuits
    d) the founding of IBM
    e) the invention high-level programming languages

4. High-level programming languages first came into use in:
    a) first generation computers
    b) second generation computers
    c) third generation computers
    d) fourth generation computers
    e) fifth generation computers

5. The operating system was a development which came into use with:
    a) first generation computers
    b) second generation computers
    c) third generation computers
    d) fourth generation computers
    e) fifth generation computers

6. CPU stands for:
    a) central printer unit
    b) central processing unit
    c) commercial processor unit
    d) commercial printer unit
    e) character printer unit

7. Which of the following are input devices for a computer system?
    a) monitor
    b) printer
    c) modem
    d) sound
    e) video
    f) keyboard

8. Which of the following are output devices for a computer system?
   a) scanner
   b) digital camera
   c) modem
   d) sound
   e) hard disk
   f) optical drives

9. The working memory of the computer system is:
   a) the hard disk
   b) the RAM
   c) the floppy disk
   d) the CD-ROM
   e) the CPU

10. Which of the following devices is the 'brain' of the computer system?
    a) CPU
    b) CD-ROM
    c) memory
    d) monitor
    e) hard disk

11. Peripheral devices are:
    a) part of the main computer processor
    b) distinct from the central processor and the main memory
    c) part of the main memory
    d) part of the software
    e) devices emulated in software

12. The I/O bus connects:
    a) the CPU with RAM
    b) the CPU with peripheral devices
    c) the RAM with peripheral devices
    d) the bus station with the railway station
    e) none of the above

Multiple-choice answers

1-b, 2-c, 3-a, 4-b, 5-c, 6-b, 7-c,d,e,f, 8-c,d, 9-b, 10-a, 11-b, 12-b

Chapter 2
Logic and sequencing

Chapter summary

This chapter covers Boolean algebra and binary numbers, fundamental gates and truth tables, and simple digital circuits analysis and synthesis. Both combinatorial circuits and sequential circuits are discussed. Finite State Machines (FSM) are introduced as vehicles for sequential circuit design.

Learning outcomes

After studying this chapter you should aim to test your achievement of the following outcomes by answering the questions at the end of the chapter. You should be able to do the following:

Outcome 1: **Understand the relationship between the denary and binary number systems, how to represent denary integers as binary numbers and why the binary number system is used in computer systems.**

Outcome 2: **Recognise the symbols of the basic logic gates and define by means of truth tables the basic logic operations.**

Outcome 3: **Use basic identities of Boolean algebra for manipulating logic expressions.**

Outcome 4: **Analyse the functionality of simple digital circuits by using truth tables and synthesise simple digital circuits starting from their truth table.**

Outcome 5: **Have an understanding of the major combinatorial and sequential functional blocks and their possible uses within the computer system.**

Outcome 6: **Be familiar with the basic concepts of finite state machines and their role in the design of sequential functional blocks.**

How will you be assessed on this?

Assessment is likely to be centred on your understanding of definitions and number conversion rules. You may also be assessed on your ability to use Boolean operators and their respective truth tables and logic gate symbols associated with these operators. Also, your ability to analyse such circuits using a truth table approach and your ability of recognising their function, given their corresponding Boolean expression and/or gate diagram may be assessed. Finally, assessment is also likely to concentrate on your understanding of functionality of the fundamental sequential circuits and your ability to analyse such circuits using a state table approach.

Useful information sources

Knapp, S. (1997) *Frequently-Asked Questions (FAQ) About Programmable Logic*, OptiMagic™, Inc, http://www.optimagic.com/faq.html#Top

Section 1

The binary number system

The binary, octal and hexadecimal number systems are introduced.

The binary number system

Our present system of numbers is based on ten separate symbols (0, . . .,9) and is called the denary (sometimes, incorrectly, the decimal system) number system. A single place that can hold numerical values between 0 and 9 is called a digit. Digits are normally combined together in groups, by using positional notation, to create larger numbers. That means that different digits have different 'powers', according to their position within a number.

Example 1

2875 has four digits; the 5 here is filling the '1s place', the 7 is filling the '10s place', the 8 is filling the '100s place' and the 2 is filling the '1000s place'.

The number 2875 can therefore be expressed as follows:

$$2875 = 2*1000 + 8*100 + 7*10 + 5*1$$

or, using powers of 10:

$$2875 = 2*10^3 + 8*10^2 + 7*10^1 + 5*10^0$$

Each digit is a placeholder for the next higher power of 10, starting in the first digit on the right with 10 raised to the power of 0.

The general rule for representing numbers in the denary system using positional notation is as follows:

$$a_{n-1}a_{n-2}...a_2a_1a_0 = a_{n-1}*10^{n-1} + a_{n-2}*10^{n-2} +...+ a_2*10^2 + a_1*10^1 + a_0$$

where n is the number of digits to the left of the decimal point.

─── CRUCIAL CONCEPT ───

The system used in computers for representing and processing data and information is a **binary number system**, or base-2 number system. Any number can be represented using the two symbols 0 and 1, by using the same positional notation as in the denary system, for example 1101_2 (the subscript indicates the base in which the number is given).

But how does one figure out what the value of the binary number 1101_2 is? In fact it works in the same way as Example 1. The procedure is shown in Example 2.

Example 2

$$1101_2 = 1*2^3 + 1*2^2 + 0*2^1 + 1*2^0 = 8 + 4 + 0 + 1 = 13_{10}$$

Each binary digit holds the value of increasing powers of 2, from the right to the left.

─── CRUCIAL CONCEPT ───

A binary digit is called a bit (short for Binary digIT).

Example 3
Counting in binary

Binary and denary numbers

Denary	Binary
0	0
1	1
2	10
3	11
4	100
5	101
6	110
7	111
8	1000

Note that, in the first two lines of the table, the numbers 0 and 1 are the same for the binary and denary systems. On the third line, at number 2 in denary, carrying takes place in binary: if a bit is 1 and one adds 1 to it, the bit becomes 0 and the next bit to the left becomes 1. Two bits are necessary to represent the numbers from 0 to 3, three bits for 0 to 7 and so on.

CRUCIAL TIP

How many **bits** are needed? The general rule is: *with n bits one can represent the numbers from 0 to (2^n-1).*

In computer systems, a group of 8 bits is called a byte or octet. Following the rule above, a byte can represent numbers from 0 to 255. Bytes are frequently used to hold individual characters in a text document. In the ASCII character set, each binary value between 0 and 127 is given a specific character. The other 128 values handle special things like accented characters from common foreign languages.

To represent lots of bytes, the following prefixes are used:

$$\text{Kilo } 1K = 2^{10} = 1024$$
$$\text{Mega } 1M = 2^{20} = 1,048,576$$
$$\text{Giga } 1G = 2^{30} = 1,073,741,824$$

1Kbyte is about 1000 bytes, 1Mbyte is about one million bytes and 1 Gbyte is about 1 billion bytes.

The octal and hexadecimal number systems

The octal (base-8) and hexadecimal (base-16) number systems provide a convenient shorthand representation for multibit numbers in a digital system, as their bases are powers of 2. The octal number system needs 8 digits; it uses digits 0-7 of the decimal system. The hexadecimal number system needs 16 digits; it uses digits 0-9 and the letters A-F. In representing multibit numbers, a string of three bits can take eight different combinations, so each 3-bit string can be uniquely represented by an octal digit. Likewise, a 4-bit string can be uniquely represented by one hexadecimal digit.

Binary, denary, octal and hexadecimal numbers

Binary	Denary	Octal	3-bit string	Hexadecimal	4-bit string
0	0	0	000	0	0000
1	1	1	001	1	0001
10	2	2	010	2	0010
11	3	3	011	3	0011
100	4	4	100	4	0100
101	5	5	101	5	0101
110	6	6	110	6	0110
111	7	7	111	7	0111
1000	8	10	-	8	1000
1001	9	11	-	9	1001
1010	10	12	-	A	1010
1011	11	13	-	B	1011
1100	12	14	-	C	1100
1101	13	15	-	D	1101
1110	14	16	-	E	1110
1111	15	17	-	F	1111

To convert a number from binary to octal, the following steps should be followed:

- start from the right end of the bit string towards the left;
- add zeroes on the left to make the total number of bits a multiple of three;
- separate the bits into groups of three;
- replace each group with the corresponding octal digit.

The procedure for binary to hexadecimal conversion is similar, except that groups of 4 bits are used and replaced.

Example 4
Convert the following binary number to octal and hexadecimal number bases.

$$11101110001011_2 = 011101110001011_2 = 011\ 101\ 110\ 001\ 011_2 = 35613_8$$
$$11101110001011_2 = 0011101110001011_2 = 0011\ 1011\ 1000\ 1011_2 = 3B8B_{16}$$

Why use the binary number system in computer systems?

Two-state circuits (also called binary) or digital, are very resistant to noise, easy to design, simple to understand and extremely reliable. Information/data can be easily manipulated by using very simple electronic circuits called gates, as will be shown in the next section.

Section 2

Boolean algebra and logic gates

This section talks about gates (the most primitive logic circuit elements used in modern computers) as hardware representations/implementations of the Boolean operators AND, OR, NOT.

Boolean algebra

In propositional logic propositions may be TRUE or FALSE and are stated as functions of other propositions which are connected by the three basic logical connectives AND, OR and NOT. An example is given below.

Example 5

The statement 'IF it is cloudy AND it is very cold THEN it will snow' is composed of the input propositions 'it is cloudy' and 'it is very cold' and has as an output the proposition 'it will snow'. The meaning of AND is that the output proposition is TRUE if and only if both input propositions are TRUE.

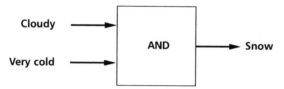

As there are only two possible values for any input proposition, we can calculate a truth value for the output proposition for all possible input combinations, as described in the following *truth table*.

Truth table for statement in Example 5

Input 1: 'it is cloudy'	Input 2: 'it is very cold'	Output: 'it will snow'
FALSE	FALSE	FALSE
FALSE	TRUE	FALSE
TRUE	FALSE	FALSE
TRUE	TRUE	TRUE

Logic propositions can be made as complex as required, by using the connectives AND, OR and NOT. Boolean algebra (developed by Boole during the 19th century) simplifies the handling of binary connectives, using ordinary algebra notation and 1 for TRUE and 0 for FALSE. In this book, the symbol * is used for AND, + for OR and $\overline{A}$ to denote NOT A.

The truth tables of the three basic binary operations are given in the table below, where A and B are the inputs and Y is the output.

Truth table of AND, OR and NOT operations

AND			OR			NOT A	
*			+			$\overline{A}$	
A	B	Y	A	B	Y	A	Y
0	0	0	0	0	0	0	1
0	1	0	0	1	1	1	0
1	0	0	1	0	1		
1	1	1	1	1	1		

These truth tables can be used to evaluate the overall truth of more complex expressions. The total number of possible input combinations in a truth table (number of lines in the table) is related to the number of inputs as follows:

CRUCIAL TIP

For n inputs, the total number of combinations will be 2^n.

A Boolean function can be transformed from an algebraic expression into a logic diagram composed of AND, OR and NOT gates. By implementing such a logic diagram in hardware, we obtain a digital circuit.

Simple gates

Digital circuits are hardware components that manipulate binary information.

The circuits are implemented using transistors within integrated circuits. Each basic circuit of transistors is referred to as a **logic gate**. This section is not concerned with the internal electronics of individual gates but only with their external logic properties; logic gates operate on one or more input binary signals to produce an output binary signal. Functionality of the logic gates and generally of digital circuits is described using truth tables.

There are seven simple gates, which in combination will implement any functional block within the computer system. Each type of gate has a name, a graphical symbol, a Boolean logic function and a truth table.

Gate name	Symbol	Logic function	Truth table

NOT (aka 'Inverter')

A————[>o——Y $Y = \overline{A}$

A	Y
0	1
1	0

AND

A————[ )——Y
B————

$Y = A*B$

A	B	Y
0	0	0
0	1	0
1	0	0
1	1	1

OR $Y = A + B$

A	B	Y
0	0	0
0	1	1
1	0	1
1	1	1

NAND (NOT AND) $Y = \overline{A * B}$

A	B	Y
0	0	1
0	1	1
1	0	1
1	1	0

NOR (NOT OR) $Y = \overline{A + B}$

A	B	Y
0	0	1
0	1	0
1	0	0
1	1	0

Exclusive OR (XOR)

('Difference') $Y = A \oplus B$

A	B	Y
0	0	0
0	1	1
1	0	1
1	1	0

Exclusive NOR (XNOR)

('Equality') $Y = \overline{A \oplus B}$

A	B	Y
0	0	1
0	1	0
1	0	0
1	1	1

Basic identities and laws of Boolean algebra

Boolean algebra facilitates the analysis and design of digital circuits. It provides a convenient tool to:

- express in algebraic form a truth table relationship between binary variables;
- express in algebraic form the input-output relationship of logic diagrams;
- find simpler circuits for the same function.

By manipulating a Boolean expression according to Boolean algebra rules, one may obtain a simpler expression that will require fewer gates for its implementation. The basic identities and laws of Boolean algebra by which these manipulations can be performed are presented below:

Commutative laws

$$A + B = B + A$$
$$A * B = B * A$$

Associative laws

$$(A + B) + C = A + (B + C) = A + B + C$$
$$A * (B * C) = (A * B) * C = A * B * C$$

19

Distributive laws

$$A * (B + C) = A * B + A * C$$

Other laws

$$A + A = A$$
$$A * A = A$$
$$A + 1 = 1$$
$$A * 1 = A$$
$$A + 0 = A$$
$$A * 0 = 0$$
$$A + \overline{A} = 1$$
$$A * \overline{A} = 0$$
$$\overline{\overline{A}} = A$$

de Morgan's law

$$\overline{(A + B)} = \overline{A} * \overline{B}$$

$$\overline{A * B} = \overline{A} + \overline{B}$$

The following example shows how Boolean algebra manipulation can be used to simplify digital circuits. Consider the circuit below.

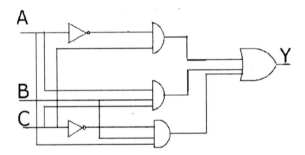

The output of the circuit can be expressed algebraically as follows:

$$Y = A * B * C + A * B * \overline{C} + \overline{A} * C$$

The expression can be simplified using the identities of Boolean algebra:

$$Y = A * B * C + A * B * \overline{C} + \overline{A} * C = A * B * (C + \overline{C}) + \overline{A} * C = A * B + \overline{A} * C$$

Note that $C + \overline{C} = 1$ and $A * B * 1 = A * B$, from the identities above. As an exercise, draw the logic diagram of the simplified circuit.

Canonical forms and circuit synthesis

A canonical form is a standard way of writing a mathematical equation. Any combinatorial circuit can be expressed in one of two canonical forms: sum-of-products ('or of ands') and product-of-sums ('and of ors'). Of the two, only the sum-of-products form is discussed here as it is the most commonly used. This canonical form is a set of Boolean equations, one for each output, in which each equation is a Boolean sum of minterms, Boolean product terms in which each input appears exactly once, either unmodified or inverted. For each input combination leading to an output of 1, the corresponding minterm must appear in the canonical expression of the Boolean function.

Consider the following truth table for a majority voter, where A, B, C are the inputs and Y is the circuit output. The output is 1 if and only if two or more of its inputs are 1.

A	B	C	Y
0	0	0	0
0	0	1	0
0	1	0	0
0	1	1	1 (minterm)
1	0	0	0
1	0	1	1 (minterm)
1	1	0	1 (minterm)
1	1	1	1 (minterm)

The canonical form for the circuit described in the above table is:

$$Y = \overline{A} * B * C + A * \overline{B} * C + A * B * \overline{C} + A * B * C$$

You can see here why the canonical form deduced is called the 'sum-of-products' form, as it reflects that the circuit function is described as a Boolean sum of the minterms, which in turn are Boolean products of the inputs. The canonical form allows the development of simple algorithms for synthesising any circuit automatically, starting from a set of Boolean equations and finishing with an integrated circuit, called a programmable logic array.

Section 3

Simple combinatorial circuits

Combinatorial circuits

CRUCIAL CONCEPT

Combinatorial circuits are logic circuits in which the output immediately reflects the state of the inputs.

For a combinatorial circuit of n input variables, there are 2^n possible input combinations. A combinatorial circuit can be specified by a truth table that lists the output values for each input variables combination, which in turn can be simply converted to a 'sum-of-products' canonical form.

From the large class of combinatorial circuits, the focus will be set in this section on several 'reusable' blocks (blocks which are used in more than one place within the hardware computer structure), which provide functions that are broadly useful. These blocks are sometimes called **functional blocks**.

Decoders

A decoder is a combinatorial circuit that converts binary information from the n coded inputs to a maximum of 2^n unique outputs (figure below). If the n-bit coded information has unused bit combinations, the decoder may have fewer than 2^n outputs.

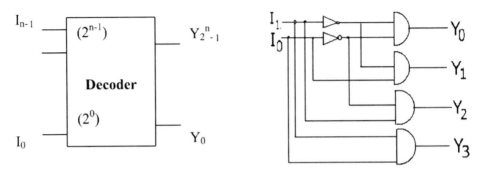

The logic diagram of a 2-to-4 decoder is shown. The two inputs are decoded into four outputs. The truth table is shown below.

I_1	I_0	Y_3	Y_2	Y_1	Y_0
0	0	0	0	0	1
0	1	0	0	1	0
1	0	0	1	0	0
1	1	1	0	0	0

Exercise

Redesign the decoder just given to include an 'enable' input, E, such that when the enable line is 0, all outputs are 0, when E is 1, the selected output is 1, as shown in the truth table below.

Inputs			Outputs			
E	I_1	I_0	Y_3	Y_2	Y_1	Y_0
0	x	x	0	0	0	0
1	0	0	0	0	0	1
1	0	1	0	0	1	0
1	1	0	0	1	0	0
1	1	1	1	0	0	0

Obtaining higher order decoders from low order ones is possible by connecting them through their enable line. For example, a 3-to-8 decoder, useful for binary-to-octal transformations, can be obtained by connecting two 2-to-4 decoders as shown below. As an exercise, check the functionality of this decoder using a truth table approach.

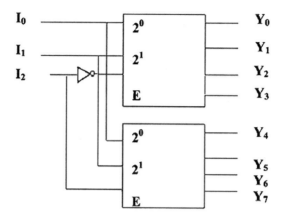

Encoders and multiplexers

An encoder is a digital circuit that performs the inverse operation of a decoder. It has 2^n (or less) input lines and n output lines. An example of an encoder is the octal-to-binary encoder, whose truth table is given in the table below. It has eight inputs, one for each of the octal digits, and three outputs that generate the corresponding binary number. It is assumed that only one input has a value of 1 at any given time.

Inputs								Outputs		
D_7	D_6	D_5	D_4	D_3	D_2	D_1	D_0	A_2	A_1	A_0
0	0	0	0	0	0	0	1	0	0	0
0	0	0	0	0	0	1	0	0	0	1
0	0	0	0	0	1	0	0	0	1	0
0	0	0	0	1	0	0	0	0	1	1
0	0	0	1	0	0	0	0	1	0	0
0	0	1	0	0	0	0	0	1	0	1
0	1	0	0	0	0	0	0	1	1	0
1	0	0	0	0	0	0	0	1	1	1

A multiplexer (MUX) is a combinatorial circuit that receives binary information from one of 2^n input data lines and directs it to a single output line, determined by a set of n selection inputs.

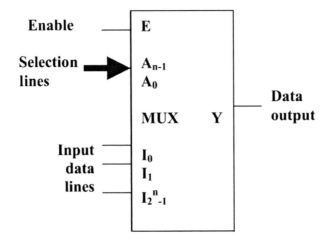

The multiplexer is also called a data selector, since it selects one of many data inputs and steers the binary information to the output.

The gates implementation and function of a 4-to-1-line multiplexer is shown below.

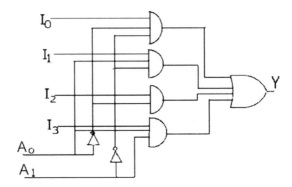

SELECT		OUTPUT
A_1	A_0	Y
0	0	I_0
0	1	I_1
1	0	I_2
1	1	I_3

As in decoders, multiplexers may have an enable input to control the operation of the unit. When the enable input is in an inactive state, the outputs are disabled, and when it is in the active state, the circuit functions as normal.

Demultiplexer

A demultiplexer is a digital circuit that performs the inverse of the multiplexing operation. A demultiplexer receives information from a single line and transmits it to one of 2^n possible output lines. The selection of the specific output is controlled by the bit combination of n selection lines.

A MUX can be used to select one of n-sources of data to transmit on a bus. At the far end of the bus, a DMUX can be used to re-route the bus data to one of m destinations.

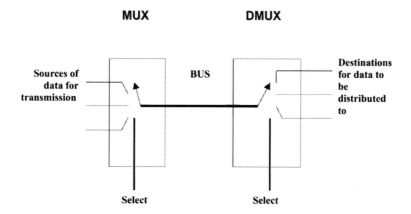

Arithmetic circuits

An arithmetic circuit is a combinatorial circuit that performs arithmetic operations such as addition, subtraction, multiplication and division, with binary numbers or with decimal numbers in a binary code.

The half adder

A combinatorial circuit that performs the addition of two bits is called a half adder. The simple addition of two bits is as follows:

$$0 + 0 = 00$$
$$0 + 1 = 01$$
$$1 + 0 = 01$$
$$1 + 1 = 10$$

The first three operations produce a sum requiring only one bit to represent, but for the fourth operation two bits are required. For this reason, two bits are always used to represent the sum of two bits: a sum bit and a carry bit.

Below is the truth table of a half adder, where X and Y are the inputs (the bits to be added) and C and S are the outputs (C – carry, S – sum).

Inputs		Outputs	
X	Y	C	S
0	0	0	0
0	1	0	1
1	0	0	1
1	1	1	0

The Boolean functions for the two outputs, obtained from the truth table, are:

$$S = (\overline{X} * Y + X * \overline{Y}) = X \oplus Y$$

$$C = X * Y$$

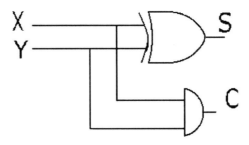

The half adder can be implemented with one XOR gate and one AND gate.

The full adder

A full adder performs the arithmetic sum of three input bits and has three inputs and two outputs. The truth table of the full adder is shown in the section below. The third input, Cin, represents the carry from the previous lower significant position. The full adder can be built from two half adders and an OR gate.

n-bit binary adder

A parallel binary adder uses n full adders in parallel, with all input bits applied simultaneously to produce the sum. The full adders are connected with the carry output from one full adder connected to the carry input of the next full adder. The more bits are there to be added, the longer it will take for the adder to complete the sum.

Inputs			Outputs	
X	Y	C_{in}	C	S
0	0	0	0	0
0	0	1	0	1
0	1	0	0	1
0	1	1	1	0
1	0	0	0	1
1	0	1	1	0
1	1	0	1	0
1	1	1	1	1

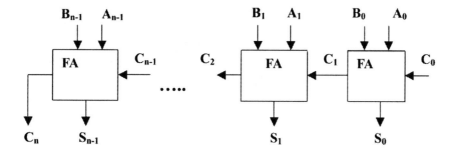

Subtractors

Subtraction circuitry can be designed by applying the same procedures as for the half and full adders. However, for the sake of modularity and blocks reuse, in practice subtraction is performed by using two's complements and full adders. Consider two integers, A and B. In order to subtract B from A, the following steps need to be performed:

- calculate (-B) by finding the two's complement of B;
- add this result to A.

The two's complement of a binary digit is found by complementing the individual bits of a number and adding one to the bottom digit.

Multiplication and division

Multiplication of two binary numbers is carried out by multiplying all combinations of individual digits and then adding them up in the appropriate positions. An example of the procedure followed for decimal and binary multiplication is shown below. Suppose one has to multiply 21 and 43.

$$21 \times 43 = 2 \times 4 \times 10^2 + 2 \times 3 \times 10^1 + 1 \times 4 \times 10^1 + 1 \times 3 \times 10^0$$

Applying the same principle for the binary two digit numbers $A = A_1A_0$ and $B = B_1B_0$, one obtains:

$$A_1A_0 \times B_1B_0 = A_1 \times B_1 \times 2^2 + A_1 \times B_0 \times 2^1 + A_0 \times B_1 \times 2^1 + A_0 \times B_0 \times 2^0$$

As all digits involved are binary ones, the multiplies can be replaced by ANDs and the multiplies by 2 can be replaced by shift right.

Division is not usually built as a combinatorial circuit. Instead, it is performed procedurally, with a sequential circuit, or in the machine code.

Section 4

Sequential logic and finite state machines (FSM)

This section discusses sequential logic circuits and their uses within the computer system. It shows how simple sequential circuits can be built from gates and gives some examples of sequential circuit design.

CRUCIAL CONCEPT

In many digital designs there is a need for logic circuits whose outputs depend not only on the present inputs, but also on the past history, or sequence of actions of the circuit. This is achievable by building memory-type circuits, which are able to store information about the past history of the circuit. Such circuits are known as **sequential logic circuits**.

One simple example of usage for such circuits is the 'traffic lights controller'.

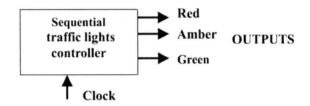

The traffic lights controller works as follows: if the colour displayed by the traffic lights is green, at the next 'clock' the lights will change to red and amber, then red and so on. The 'next' colour to be displayed depends on the colour displayed 'now'.

CRUCIAL CONCEPT

The **state** of a system is its condition at a particular moment, described by the value of its outputs or 'variables'.

The traffic lights controller requires four states, named S_0, S_1, S_2, S_3. The circuit evolves from one state to another under the control of a clock signal. Such circuits are called synchronous circuits.

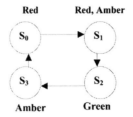

In this state diagram the arrows signify transitions from one state to another which happen only on receipt of a clock 'tick'.

A circuit with n binary state variables has 2^n possible states. As the number of possible states is always finite, sequential circuits are often called finite state machines (FSMs). The behaviour of FSMs is described by means of state tables, which contain the following columns: present state, input, next state and output. The lines of the state table contain all possible combinations of the present states and inputs.

Suppose the requirement is to design a binary counter, which counts in the sequence 0, 1, 2, 3. The first step in the design procedure is to translate the circuit specification into a state diagram. The state diagram is then converted to a state table, from which is designed the logic. As the circuit has to cope with four states, 0, 1, 2 and 3, two bits will suffice. The binary states, therefore, are: 00, 01, 10 and 11. The circuit has to change state when the clock 'ticks', and when an external input , X, equals 1 (true). When X is 0 (false), nothing will happen. These values 'label' the transition arrow to which they refer.

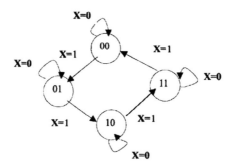

The state table can be drawn as below, with two state variables, A and B assigned to the two bits representing the states. In this example the 'X' input is the same as the clock.

Present state		Input	Next state	
A	B	X = Ck	A^+	B^+
0	0	0	0	0
0	0	1	0	1
0	1	0	0	1
0	1	1	1	0
1	0	0	1	0
1	0	1	1	1
1	1	0	1	1
1	1	1	0	0

We now look at some functional blocks which will allow us to store these states, a memory device.

Flip-flops and memory devices

CRUCIAL CONCEPT

The simplest sequential circuit is the **flip-flop** — a memory/storage element for one bit.

The flip-flop represents the basic building block for sequential circuits. According to their internal structure, there are several types of flip-flops, of which two are discussed here:

- the set-reset latch;
- the D latch.

The set–reset latch (SR)

The SR latch is a circuit constructed from two cross-coupled NOR gates. The inputs are labelled S for Set and R for Reset.

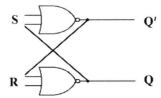

The outputs Q and $\overline{Q}$ depend not only on the inputs S and R, but also on the previous values of the outputs. Analysis of the circuit results in:

$$Q = \overline{R + Q'}$$
$$Q' = \overline{S + Q}$$

Considering each possible combination of the two input variables:

1. For S = 0, R = 0: $Q = \overline{Q'}$; $Q' = \overline{Q}$

Therefore, Q and Q' could be either 0 or 1, depending on the previous values of S and R (i.e. just before they were taken to 0).

2. For S = 0, R = 1

$$Q = \overline{1 + Q'} = \overline{1} = 0$$
$$Q' = \overline{0 + Q} = \overline{Q} = 1$$

This input condition, known as RESET, forces Q = 0 and Q' = 1.

3. For S = 1, R = 0

$$Q' = \overline{1 + Q} = \overline{1} = 0$$
$$Q = \overline{0 + Q'} = \overline{Q'} = 1$$

This is the case opposite to 2, forcing the output to the set condition Q = 1 & Q' = 0. This input condition is known as SET.

4. For S = 1, R = 1

$$Q = \overline{1 + Q'} = \overline{1} = 0$$
$$Q' = \overline{1 + Q'} = \overline{1} = 0$$

Although the outputs are stable for this input condition. If S and R are changed simultaneously to true, it is impossible to predict whether Q will remain at 0 or become 1, this is therfore an indeterminate state.

Input		Output
S	R	
1	0	Set state
0	0	
0	1	Reset state
0	0	
1	1	Indeterminate

The functionality of the S-R latch can be made synchronous by the introduction of a clock signal, to give a clocked SR flip-flop.

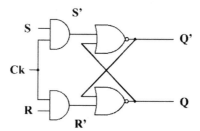

Exercise
Produce a table showing the function of the the clocked S-R.

CRUCIAL CONCEPT

The **D-type latch**, described below, is a 1 bit memory device.

The D-type latch is a special case of clocked R-S latch with R = $\overline{S}$ at all times. This new design eliminates therefore the indeterminate state (S = R = 1), which represented the drawback of the S-R latch. The latch has two inputs: D-data and Ck-clock. The output Q follows the input D, as long as the clock is at logic level 1. The output Q is 'frozen' with the value of D at the instant the clock is taken at logic level 0, that is, the latch stores the value that was on the D input.

Ck	D	Next state of Q
0	X	No change
1	0	Q = 0; Reset state
1	1	Q = 1; Set state

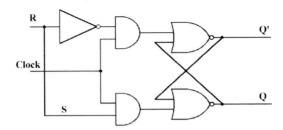

It is also possible to build flip-flops in which state changes are 'triggered' when the clock transits from 0 to 1, these are called edge-triggered devices. The output Q follows the input D, synchronising it with the transition of the clock from 0 to 1.

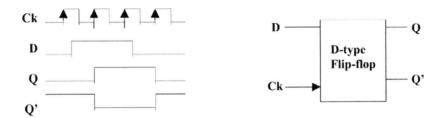

Registers

Data processing in a computer system is usually done on fixed size binary 'words'. Hence, we need devices able to store a number of bits of information at a time. A register is a device in which a number of bits (binary digits) can be stored and retrieved.

A set of n flip-flops can be used to store n bits of information, to form a register. A schematic diagram of a n-bit register and three short-hand notations are shown below. The usual convention is to number the bits from 0 to (n-1).

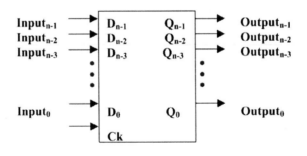

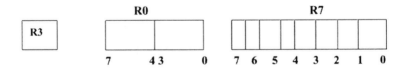

CRUCIAL CONCEPT

Registers are one of the fundamental building blocks of computer systems. They may contain data or control bits. One of the most common data manipulations involving registers is that of 'register transfer' through which the binary content of one register is copied into another register.

Using registers in sequential logic

We now return to the counter example. We have already described the state diagram and the state table. We will use a D-type register to store the state of the machine. The next state will be generated using combinatorial logic from the current state and will form the inputs to the register, as shown below.

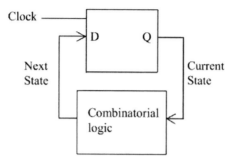

We add two more columns to the state table, for the inputs of the two flip-flops. The X input (the clock) has been implicitly considered here. The excitations (DA and DB respectively) are filled in by matching the required value for the input D of a flip-flop with the transition which has to take place. In this case, in order for the circuit to proceed from state AB = 00 to state A + B + = 01, DA = 0 = A + and DB = 1 = B + .

Present state		Next state		Flip-flop 1	Flip-flop 2
A	B	A^+	B^+	D_A	D_B
0	0	0	1	0	1
0	1	1	0	1	0
1	0	1	1	1	1
1	1	0	0	0	0

The expressions for the 'next state' $A^+ B^+ = D_A D_B$ can be obtained using sum-of-products procedures:

$$D_A = \overline{A} * B + A * \overline{B} = A \oplus B$$
$$D_B = \overline{A} * \overline{B} + A * \overline{B} = \overline{B}$$

The resulting circuit implementation is as follows.

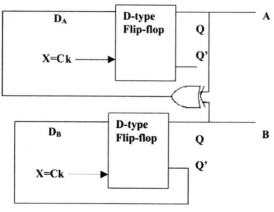

Section 5

End of chapter assessment

Exercises

1. Simplify the following expressions using Boolean algebra identities and laws:

$$A * B * C * (A * B * \overline{C} + A * \overline{B} * C + \overline{A} * B * C)$$

$$A * B + \overline{A} * C + A * \overline{B} + \overline{A} * \overline{C}$$

2. The circuit below can be represented by a single gate. Which?

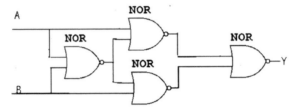

3. Determine the expression for Y in the figure below:

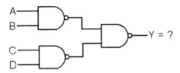

Multiple-choice questions

1. The denary number 172 is represented in binary as:
    a) 10101100
    b) 00110101
    c) 10101010
    d) 11001100
    e) 11100111

2. What is the main reason for the use of binary logic in computer systems?
    a) robustness against noise
    b) parallel processing of data
    c) less wiring
    d) smaller computers
    e) convention

3. What is the minimum number of bits required to represent all the characters on a keyboard that had nine keys:
    a) 1
    b) 2
    c) 3
    d) 4
    e) 5

4. What is the minimum number of bits required to represent all the characters on a keyboard that has 22 keys?
   a) 1
   b) 2
   c) 3
   d) 4
   e) 5

5. The XOR function can be expressed in terms of AND, OR and NOT as:
   a) $(\overline{A} * \overline{B}) + (A * B)$

   b) $(\overline{A} * B) + (A * \overline{B})$

   c) $(\overline{A} * A) + (B * B)$

   d) $(\overline{A} + B) * (A + \overline{B})$

   e) $((A * \overline{B}) * A) + \overline{B}$

6. The result of regrouping the following expression,

   $Y = ((A * B * C) * (A * \overline{B})) + ((A + B) + A) + (\overline{A} + (\overline{A} * B))$

   is:
   a) Y = A
   b) Y = B
   c) Y = 0
   d) Y = 1
   e) Y = tri-state

7. A binary digit is called:
   a) byte
   b) bit
   c) word
   d) and
   e) or

8. A demultiplexer has:
   a) one input and multiple outputs
   b) one output and multiple inputs
   c) one input, one output
   d) multiple inputs and multiple outputs
   e) none of the above

9. A multiplexer has:
   a) one input and multiple outputs
   b) one output and multiple inputs
   c) one input, one output
   d) multiple inputs and multiple outputs
   e) none of the above

10. The number of state variables needed for the design of a FSM with six possible states is:
    a) 1
    b) 2
    c) 3
    d) 4
    e) 5

11. Consider the FSM in the figure below.

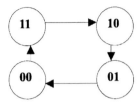

It represents the functionality of a:

a) synchronous counter in the sequence 0-1-2-3
b) asynchronous counter in the sequence 0-1-2-3
c) synchronous counter in the sequence 3-2-1-0
d) asynchronous counter in the sequence 3-2-1-0
e) synchronous counter in the sequence 3-2-3-0

Multiple-choice answers

1-a, 2-a, 3-d, 4-e, 5-b, 6-d, 7-d, 8-a, 9-b, 10-c, 11-c

Chapter 3
Computer system components

Chapter summary

This chapter discusses the four main components of a computer system: the processor, the buses, the memory and the I/O devices. An introduction to instructions, sequencing and system software is provided to aid the understanding of role and functionality of the central processing unit (CPU).

Learning outcomes

After studying this chapter you should aim to test your achievement of the following outcomes by answering the multiple-choice questions at the end of the chapter. You should be able to do the following:

Outcome 1: Enumerate the major computer system components.
Outcome 2: Understand the way these components are interconnected and the way they communicate in order to perform tasks.
Outcome 3: Explain the role of components such as the ALU, control unit, buses and interfaces within the computer system.
Outcome 4: Differentiate between the main types of data (instructions and data) and explain how instructions are fetched and executed.
Outcome 5: Recognise the main memory types within the computer system and define their role.
Outcome 6: Analyse, at logic diagram level, the functionality of a memory cell of one bit.

How will you be assessed on this?

You will need to understand how data and program instructions are represented internally, stored, accessed and processed. Also, understanding of the role and types of memory and its operation and the I/O devices and their interfacing may be assessed. Knowledge of the registers and components involved is essential, as is the succession of operations.

Useful information sources

Ars Technica LLC (1998) *Ars Technica: The Ars Technopaedia*, http://arstechnica.com/paedia/
Karbo, M. B., (1996) *Hardware Guides*, http://www.karbosguide.com/
PC Tech Guide, http://www.pctechguide.com

Section 1

The central processing unit

This section discusses the main components of a computer system, the Central Processing Unit (CPU).

The central processing unit (CPU)

In a computer system the CPU is fabricated on a silicon chip which is encapsulated in a package surrounded by terminals (pins), connected to the electrical inputs and outputs of the chip. The packaged device is called a microprocessor. CPUs have for many years doubled their performance about every 18 months. (This is known as Moore's Law after its exposition by the vice-president of Intel, Thomas Moore.) There are no indications that this trend will stop.

Functioning of the CPU

The CPU continually receives instructions to be executed. The CPU's work itself consists mostly of calculations and data transport.

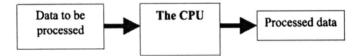

Types of data

The CPU is fed binary data via the system bus (see below). The CPU receives two types of data:

- instructions (program code) which tell it what to do with the data;
- data, which must be handled according to the instructions.

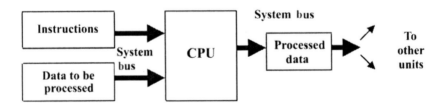

CRUCIAL CONCEPT

An **instruction** is an elementary operation in a programming language. It is the smallest command that a programmer can give to a computer. The way the different operations are encoded into binary numbers is called the **instruction format**.

Any instruction contains two types of information:

- what has to be done by the instruction (for example adding, subtracting, storing data, printing), called the **operation code**;
- with what data to do it, called the **data field**.

The format in which instructions are stored internally is known as machine code or machine language. Each microprocessor has its own machine language. An example of an instruction in machine code is given below.

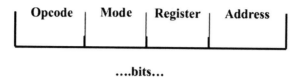

....bits...

In this particular example:

- the **opcode** field specifies the operation;
- the **address** field designates the memory (RAM) address of the first operand involved in the instruction;
- the **register** field specifies an operand in a register;
- the **mode** field selects from the various types of operands that the machine language permits.

System software

Higher level languages make the programmer's job easier and give a closer correspondence between the objects and operations of the language and of the application.

In order for the machine to execute a high-level language program (such as programs in C, Java, etc), the program has to be converted into a form that the computer understands before execution can commence. The two options for conversion are:

- compilation or translation, in which the high level program is compiled into a machine code form, which is stored and executed when required;
- interpretation, in which a machine code program is used to read the high-level instructions and perform the operations which they specify.

The work of the CPU is:

- decoding instructions;
- retrieving and restoring the data to be operated on;
- performing the required calculations.

From the hardware point of view, the main components of the CPU are: the ALU, the control unit and registers.

CRUCIAL CONCEPT

The **arithmetic-logic unit** (ALU) performs arithmetic and logical operations on input data.

A full adder can be extended as shown below to allow subtracting, multiplying, dividing integers and also for performing logic bit by bit operations and is known as the arithmetic and logic unit (ALU). In a modern processor this section of the computer system will use a small portion of a microprocessor chip.

A simple four function ALU controlled by two lines [with a two to four decoder]
The functions are A AND B   A OR B   NOT B   and A + B

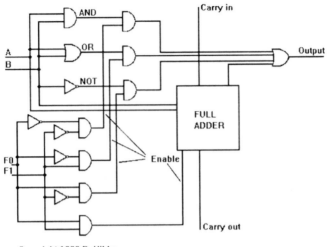

Copyright 1998 D. Hibbs

The ALU communicates with the computer's memory where the operands are stored. To speed up the operation some computers have several (eight to 128, depending on the processor architecture) faster memory locations, called registers, within the CPU.

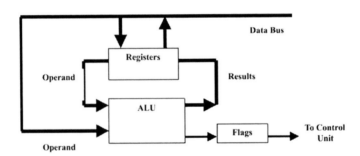

Within the computer system, the operation of the ALU is directed by the control unit. ALU operations occur when it is provided with the correct sequence of input signals by the control unit. The operation performed may depend on the results of a previous operation. This is achieved using the 'flag register' or 'status register' which stores information about the result of the last ALU operation (for example, whether it resulted in a zero result, negative result, or produced a carry and/or an overflow).

A simple block diagram of an ALU is shown below.

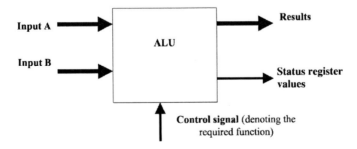

The inputs and the outputs of the ALU will typically be 8, 16 or 32 bits wide. The control signal consists of a number of bits, depending upon the number of functions which the ALU is capable of performing, which may include:

- addition/subtraction;
- multiplication/division (only in large computer systems);
- logical tests (eg: tests to see if the result of an operation is zero);
- logical tests for zero (tests if an operand has all bits zero);
- bitwise AND of two operands;
- bitwise OR of two operands;
- bit shifting;
- comparator function (>, <, =).

CRUCIAL CONCEPT

The **control unit** manages the execution of programs. Each instruction to be executed is brought in sequence to the control unit, where it is decoded and orders are issued to various parts of the system resulting in the sequence of operations necessary to perform the operation.

Once an instruction has been executed, the control unit fetches the next instruction. A simplified diagram of the control unit is given below.

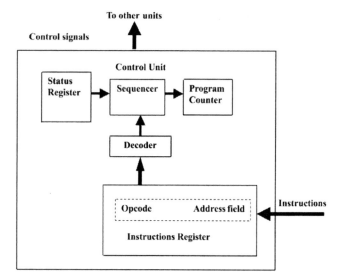

The role of various control unit components is given below:

- The instruction register holds the instruction to be executed.
- The decoder decodes the instruction. The decoded information is sent to the sequencer.
- The sequencer sends out the appropriate control signals. The timing is determined by the system's internal clock. (Quartz clocks in current microprocessors run at frequencies above 1000MHz. The faster the clock, the quicker the central processor.)
- The status (flag) register provides the sequencer with details of previous operations results.
- The program counter (also sometimes called instruction pointer) points to the memory location of the 'next instruction', and is incremented as each instruction is processed.

Section 2

Buses, memory and I/O devices

This section discusses the three other essential components of the computer system (i.e. the buses, the memory and the I/O devices).

The buses

The buses transmit data between different components. The buses connect the CPU to all the other components. The CPU receives and sends its data from and to two kinds of bus:

- the system bus, which connects the CPU with RAM;
- the I/O buses, which connect the CPU with other components.

The system bus connects to the I/O buses, the CPU with RAM and maybe a buffer memory as shown below (this is a simplification, modern bus systems are much more complex). It is designed to match a specific type of CPU: the processor technology determines the dimension of the system bus, how fast it is and the control signals it uses.

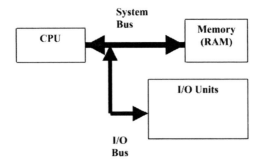

The I/O buses move data. They connect all I/O devices with the system bus, and therefore to the CPU and RAM. I/O devices are those components which can receive or send data (disk drives, monitor, keyboard, etc). There may be more than one I/O bus on a computer, and they may be standardised to allow easy addition of components. I/O bus standards are discussed in Chapter 6.

A bus can be divided into three major sections.

- The data bus: a section which carries the data, which might consist of 8 to 64 bits wires, where one wire can carry 1 bit of data per operation. This is known as the 'bus width'.
- The address bus: a number of wires that indicate the address of the data to be accessed. This bus is usually unidirectional, the addresses being sent in one direction only, from the CPU to other devices.
- The control bus: provides information about the how the data on the bus is to be transferred.

One convention to represent a bus uses a single line with a slash to indicate that there are actually a number of wires.

Since several units within the computer system share the same bus lines, there is a need for interface procedures for bused modules to insure that, for instance, two modules do not attempt to write data on the bus in the same time and to identify the module for which the data are intended.

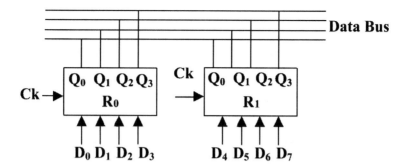

Consider two registers connected to the data bus (four bit registers are shown above). Such a configuration generates a bus conflict. The outputs of ordinary gates or components must not be connected together.

If, for instance the output Q_0 of R_0 was 1, while the corresponding output of R_1 was 0, since they are connected to the same wire, we have connected logic 1 and logic 0 together. The result is an indeterminate logic level and a state which might damage the output circuitry of the registers.

One solution to the conflict problem is to connect only the output lines of one register at a time to the data bus. This is achieved by inserting a special type of buffer circuit, known as a three-state or tristate buffer, which has a built-in switch which can disconnect the output itself from the output connection, into each output line of the registers. Such a buffer has the truth table and the symbol shown below.

Truth table for a three state buffer

Input	Enable	Output
0	1	0
1	1	1
0	0	Not connected
1	0	Not connected

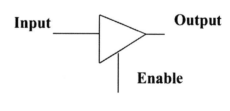

If the enable line is active (1), then the tri-state buffer behaves like an ordinary buffer: the 'switch' is closed and the output logic state is the same as the input. However, if the enable line is not active (0), then the 'switch' is open and effectively there is no connection between the register output lines and the data bus. Such a state is known as 'high impedance'. Thus, each output line in each register has a tri-state buffer controlled by the enable control line. Only one register enable line must be true at any one time.

CRUCIAL CONCEPT

The **memory** is an esential to computer systems as it is needed for storing programs and data. A memory unit is a collection of storage cells together with associated circuits, needed to transfer information in and out of the storage.

Memory organisation and capacity

The memory stores binary information in groups of bits called words. A word in memory is the maximum package of bits that is moved in and out of storage as a unit, and is typically subdivided into 8-bit 'bytes'. Every word is the same size (between 16 and 64 bits) independent of the type of data it holds. A memory word or byte may represent a number, an instruction code, one or more alphanumeric characters, or any other binary coded information.

The internal structure of a memory unit is determined by the number of words it contains and the number of bits in each word. Input lines, called address lines, connected to internal decoders select one particular word. The unique identification number for each memory word, the **address**, starts from 0 and continues up to (2^m-1), where m is the number of address lines.

In each word the bits are numbered from right to left (the most significant bit is the leftmost one). We must carefully distinguish between a storage location's address and its content.

The capacity of a particular computer's memory – that is, the number of words available – is called the **memory size**, the size of addresses gives the **address space**. If we allow m bits to hold a binary address then the address space is 2^m and the addresses range from 0 to (2^m-1). Since address spaces are usually fairly large, they are often expressed in Kbytes or Mbytes.

Example
A computer with a 256 Kbytes memory has 2^{18} = 262,144 addressable locations.

The basic memory structure

The basic operations on a memory are READ and WRITE. Since basic memory operations are concerned with one word, the address of this word is presented to the memory with the READ/WRITE control signal(s). The operations Read and Write act on one word of data and hence a data route of one word wide must be provided to the memory.

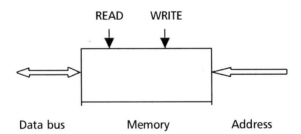

Data bus   Memory   Address

Internally the memory consists of a large array of registers. The inputs are connected to the data bus, and data latched into that particular register when it is selected by the address decoder simultaneously with the READ signal. The outputs are connected to a data selector (multiplexor), which is connected to the data bus (via a three-state buffer). The data from the addressed cell is selected by the data selector, while the READ signal enables the selected data onto the bus.

Example
RAM chips come in a variety of sizes. An example of such a chip appears at the top of the facing page.

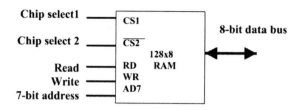

Here, the chip has 128 locations, each location holding an 8-bit word. The locations are addressable through the 7-bit wide address bus (7 bits are necessary in order to address $128 = 2^7$ locations). The chip communicates with the CPU through an 8-bit data bus (which matches the word length in each location). The communication is bi-directional, as data can either be Read from the memory (and sent to the CPU) or Written to memory (in which case data is coming from the CPU). The memory operation is specified by the two input lines Read and Write. There are also two control input lines, on each RAM chip (Chip select 1 and Chip select 2), which enable the chip only when it is selected by the CPU. Whilst CS1 is 'active high' (1 to select), CS2 is 'active low' (0 to select), as indicated by the inverter sign on its symbol. There is a good reason for having two control lines rather than one on each RAM chip: they allow the simple decoding of the address lines when there are multiple RAM chips within the system.

Two major types of memory are used in computer systems: random access memory (RAM) and read-only memory (ROM).

CRUCIAL CONCEPTS

In **random access memory** (RAM), the memory cells can be accessed for information transfer from any desired random location. The process of locating a word in such a memory is identical no matter where the cells are located within the physical memory. An equal amount of time is required to locate any word. Both Read and Write operations, as described above, can be performed on RAMs.

Read only memory (ROM) is a memory unit that allows the Read operation only. The data in a ROM cannot be altered by a program. ROMs have random access characteristics and their content is not lost when the power is switched off.

I/O devices

No computer system is complete without a range of I/O devices or peripherals. Programs and data need to be entered into the computer's memory, and results obtained from processing and computation must be recorded or displayed (or both) for the user. I/O involves a very large part of the computer.

Common examples of I/O devices are: the keyboard, printers, the mouse, magnetic disks and CD-ROMs. Peripheral devices themselves will to be discussed in Chapter 6. Here we concentrate on the communication and data transfer between them and the CPU. As peripheral devices are often electromechanical, and the CPU and the memory are electronic, interfacing between them is necessary in order for them to communicate. The CPU and peripherals work at different speeds, so a synchronisation mechanism is also needed.

Specialised interface logic is placed between the CPU bus and a peripheral device. In addition, each device may have its own controller to monitor and control its operation (these are often called 'intelligent' or 'smart' devices). The CPU communicates with the memory and an I/O device in the same way, transferring data through a bus, although it is likely to be an I/O bus for devices, as shown in the diagram.

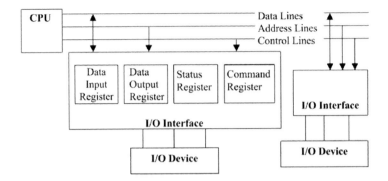

- A particular I/O device is selected through the delivery of its address on the address line of the I/O bus.
- Once a peripheral has identified its address on the bus, it becomes active.
- The interface of the device reads the function code provided by the CPU on the control lines of the I/O bus and responds to it.

There are four types of function codes an interface may receive and execute:

- Control command: issued to activate a peripheral and inform it what to do.
- Status: used to test various status conditions in the interface and the peripheral.
- Output data: causes the interface to respond by transferring data from the bus to its data output register. The outputs of this register connect to the data lines of the I/O device.
- Input data: causes the interface to receive a data item from the I/O device and place it in its data input register.

The registers within the interface of an I/O device are called I/O registers or I/O ports.

Instructions and sequencing

This brief section explains the instruction cycle in the computer system.

The instruction cycle

For the purposes of this discussion, we will consider a simple processor, illustrated below.

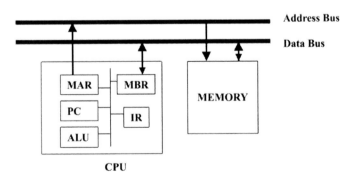

Its 'instruction cycle' (the sequence of steps performed for every instruction) is divided into two parts, the fetch cycle and the execute cycle.

Fetch cycle   1. Fetch the next instruction from memory to the control unit.

                2. Decode the instruction.

Execute cycle   3. Fetch operands and process the instruction.

                4. Write the result back.

The fetch cycle is identical for all instructions within the computer. The execution cycle depends on the particular instruction being executed. Hence, there will be as many different execution cycles as there are instructions defined for that particular computer. Instructions typically fall into several groups:

- the arithmetic and logic groups (add, subtract, multiply, etc, AND, OR, XOR);
- 'move' or 'copy' operations which provide a means of transferring information from memory location to memory location and between memory and I/O devices;
- control operations, which modify the instruction flow through the program, often conditionally on the result of a previous operation, by forcing the next instruction to be obtained from somewhere else in memory.

The timing signals for performing the steps within the instruction cycle originate from the control unit of the CPU.

The fetch cycle

For an instruction to be fetched from memory, the following operations have to be performed:

1. Load the contents of the program counter (PC) into the memory address register (MAR) which is then put onto the address bus.
2. Instruct the memory to perform a read operation which will result in data being placed on the data bus.
3. Store the value on the data bus in the memory buffer register (MBR) in the CPU.
4. Transfer the value in the MBR into the instruction register (IR).
5. Increment the contents of the program counter.

The execute cycle

The execute cycle differs from instruction to instruction. For example, consider the instruction ADD which adds the contents of a named register to the accumulator and leaves the result in the accumulator. Since the registers reside in the CPU, the execution sequence would be:

- transfer the accumulator contents to the ALU via the internal bus;
- transfer the addressed register contents to the other ALU input, via the internal bus;
- signal the ALU to add;
- store the results in the accumulator.

Section 4

End of chapter assessment

Multiple-choice questions

1. Suppose the opcode field of an instruction contains 4 bits. Further, suppose the instructions are uniquely defined by their opcode. The instruction set in this case will contain a maximum of:
    a) 4 instructions
    b) 8 instructions
    c) 16 instructions
    d) 32 instructions
    e) 64 instructions

2. The ALU performs the following function:
    a) communicates with the I/O devices
    b) performs the arithmetic and logic operations
    c) performs the memory transfer operations
    d) stores data
    e) fetches instructions

3. The flags associated with the ALU store:
    a) information about the result of the last ALU operation
    b) the results of the last ALU operation
    c) control signals for other components of the CPU
    d) the memory address of the ALU data
    e) the country of origin of the computer

4. The number of bits in the control signal necessary for an ALU with 25 operations is:
    a) 25   d) 1
    b) 4   e) 0
    c) 5

5. Within the CPU, the role of the control unit is to:
    a) manage the execution of programs
    b) perform arithmetic and logic operations
    c) send control signals to the CPU
    d) send control signals to peripherals
    e) store data

6. Three-state buffers are used to:
    a) interface memory locations
    b) interface I/O devices
    c) interface components connected to the buses
    d) store ternary numbers
    e) provide an extra logic state

7. The I/O bus connects:
    a) the CPU with RAM
    b) the I/O devices with the CPU and RAM
    c) the RAM with the I/O devices
    d) the I with the O
    e) the input with the output

8. The data bus is:
   a) unidirectional
   b) bi-directional
   c) bi-sexual
   d) bicycle
   e) unicycle

9. The address bus is:
   a) unidirectional
   b) bi-directional
   c) bi-sexual
   d) bicycle
   e) unicycle

10. The following memory is specified by the number of words times the number of bits per word. How many address lines are needed for a 2G X 8 memory?
    a) 30
    b) 31
    c) 21
    d) 20
    e) 36

11. The following memory is specified by the number of words times the number of bits per word. How many data lines are needed for a 2G X 8 memory?
    a) 2G
    b) 8
    c) 2
    d) 30
    e) 1

12. Give the number of bytes stored in a 16M X 32 memory:
    a) 2^{20}
    b) 2^{22}
    c) 2^{24}
    d) 2^{26}
    e) 2^{30}

13. Random access memory is a type of memory which:
    a) can only be written to
    b) can only be read
    c) can be written and read
    d) has random contents
    e) gives random outputs

14. Within an I/O interface, the status register is used:
    a) to store commands for the peripherals, from the CPU
    b) to store data received from the CPU
    c) to signal to the CPU if the I/O device is ready for data transfer
    d) to prepare data to be transferred from the I/O device to the CPU
    e) to prepare data to be transferred from the CPU to the I/O device

15. The fetch cycle implies amongst others:
    a) decoding an instruction
    b) obeying an instruction
    c) executing an instruction
    d) both decoding and obeying an instruction
    e) writing the result

Multiple-choice answers

1-c, 2-b, 3-a, 4-c, 5-a, 6-c, 7-b, 8-b, 9-a, 10-b, 11-b, 12-d, 13-c, 14-c, 15-a

Chapter 4
Memory systems

Chapter summary

The characteristics of different memory devices are presented, along with the choices and trade-offs involved in the design of a memory system and the memory management required for large systems.

Learning outcomes

After studying this chapter you should aim to test your achievement of the following outcomes by answering the multiple-choice questions at the end of the chapter. You should be able to do the following:

Outcome 1: Explain the concepts of central memory and auxiliary memory.
Outcome 2: List the properties of central and auxiliary memories.
Outcome 3: Justify the need for memory hierarchy in computer systems.
Outcome 4: Explain the role of various memory components within the memory hierarchy of the computer system.
Outcome 5: Describe the various types of memory devices such as semiconductor memories, disks and tapes.

How will you be assessed on this?

Assessment will be centred on your understanding of the concepts behind the 'hierarchy of memory' and the physical structure of memory devices, their block diagrams and logical signals. You also need to know what type of storage device to use in different situations.

Useful information sources

SCSI trade association, technical information on storage devices, http://www.scsita.org/

Section 1

The memory hierarchy

This section explains the concept of memory hierarchy. The key properties of memory devices are presented and the trade-offs needed for building an efficient memory system are explained.

The memory system

At system level, one can distinguish two broad classes of memory in computer systems:

- central memory, which is the working memory of the computer;
- auxiliary memory, also known as secondary memory or backing store.

Both memory types share the following key properties:

- Speed: expressed in terms of access time (the average time required to reach a storage location in memory and obtain its contents) and cycle time (determines how fast one can access memory on a continuous basis, including the time needed for 'recovery' after an access).
- Type of access: whether the data can be accessed directly or only after passing over other data.
- Density and capacity: indicate how many bits can be stored per memory unit.
- Volatility: represents the length of time for which the memory is capable of retaining the data in a readable form. A magnetic disk memory, for example, is non-volatile whereas the semiconductor memory of a computer is often volatile (i.e. will lose its contents at power switch off).
- Component cost: usually measured as the cost per bit; as a general rule, the faster a memory device is, the more expensive.
- Power dissipation: has reliability and cost implications.

Overall, the performance of a computer system is related directly to its execution time. The execution time is given by:

$$CPU\ time = IC * CPI * Clock\ period$$

where IC is the number of instructions executed and CPI is the average number of clock cycles required per instruction (we will discuss this concept further in Chapter 5). The performance of a computer depends on the interface between the processor and the memory. If this interface is not correct, a significant increase in CPI can result. There are two parameters which characterise the processor-memory interface.

CRUCIAL CONCEPT

Memory bandwidth is the rate at which the memory sytem can service requests from the processor multiplied by the width (in bits) of the memory.

Memory latency is the time between the initiation of a memory request and its completion.

System speed is dominated by memory performance.

We can summarise the difference between the two broad classes of memory as follows:

	Advantages	Disadvantages
Central memory	Fast	Often volatile
	Physically small	Expensive
	Directly addressable	Small capacity
Auxiliary memory	Inexpensive	Bulky
	Non-volatile	Slow
	Large capacity	

The performance/price trade-off

The faster the processor, the faster the data and programs have to be accessed and delivered. A perfect memory system would be one that can supply immediately any data that the CPU requests. However, the three characteristics of memories, capacity, speed and cost are in direct opposition. A speed-cost trade-off is commonly performed when designing computer systems.

CRUCIAL CONCEPT

Modern computer systems tackle the issue of price-performance trade-off by implementing a **memory hierarchy** organised into several levels, each smaller, faster and more expensive per byte than the next. The goal is to provide a memory system with cost almost as low as the cheapest level of memory and speed almost as fast as the fastest level.

The concept of memory hierarchy takes advantage of two principles:

- the principle of temporal locality of reference – accessed memory words are likely to be accessed again quickly;
- the principle of spatial locality states – if a memory word is accessed, adjacent words are likely to be accessed soon afterwards.

At a given stage of technology the fastest memories have lower density and cost substantially more per bit. The memory hierarchies of modern general purpose computers generally contain the following:

- registers – the smallest, fastest memory;
- cache memory;
- main memory;
- virtual memory;
- auxiliary memory – the largest, slowest memory.

A given memory access is handled by the fastest memory available holding the required data. The principles of locality ensure that accesses to the larger, slower memories are relatively less frequent. Components of the memory hierarchy and their communication with other subsystems within the computer are shown below.

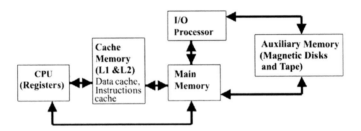

The components of the hierarchy are discussed below.

CRUCIAL CONCEPT

Registers are the small, fast storage buffers within the CPU. The compiler (which will be discussed in more detail in the following chapters) is responsible for managing their use, deciding which values should be kept in the available register at each point in the execution of a program.

Cache is small, very-high-speed memory located close to the CPU, that holds the most recently accessed code or data. This memory increases the speed of processing by making the current programs and data available to the CPU quickly.

By inserting cache memory between the CPU and the main memory and using it for storing temporary data frequently needed in present calculations and the programs currently being executed, the processing speed can be considerably increased. (The cache memory may have an access time five to ten times smaller than the access time of the main memory and its speed approaches the speed of the CPU components.) The success of cache in speeding up the processor is due to the locality of reference property of programs.

Its operation is as follows:

- when the CPU needs to access the memory, the cache is examined first;
- if the necessary information was found in the cache, it is read by the CPU;
- if the necessary information was not found in the cache, the main memory is accessed;
- a block of words, amongst which is the word needed, is transferred from the main memory to the cache.

When the CPU finds the requested data item in the cache, it is called a **cache hit**. When it doesn't, it results in a **cache miss**, and the data must be fetched from main memory. The ratio of the number of hits divided by the total number of CPU references to memory (hits and misses) is called the **hit ratio**. (Some computer architectures have a hit ratio as high as 0.9.) Caches can vary widely in their size and organisation, and there may be more than one level of cache in the hierarchy. Many of the present day caches have a two level structure, with the level closer to the processor called L1 cache and the next level called L2.

CRUCIAL CONCEPT

The **main memory** occupies a central position by being able to communicate both directly with the CPU and with the auxiliary memory through the I/O processor. It is relatively fast and it is used to store programs and data during the computer operation. Main memory satisfies the demand of caches and serves, together with the I/O processor, as the interface with the auxiliary memory.

Virtual memory is a system whereby auxiliary storage devices can be made to appear to be additional main memory, so far as the program is concerned.

Virtual memory is used to give the appearance of a memory much larger than the main memory. This is achieved by creating a virtual address space, so that each program will 'see' a memory the size of the virtual address space. Within this virtual address space, main memory acts as a cache to a memory image stored on the auxiliary memory. Virtual memory relies on support both of hardware (the memory management unit – MMU) and software, which map each virtual address for each program into a physical, real address. More information on this is given in Chapter 8.

CRUCIAL CONCEPT

When programs or data not residing in the main memory are needed by the CPU, they are brought in from the **auxiliary memory**. Auxiliary memory holds those parts of the programs and data that are not presently used by the CPU. It should be noted that the CPU has no direct access to the auxiliary memory. The auxiliary memory is much slower, having an access time 1000 times larger than the main memory.

The most common auxiliary memory devices used in computer systems are magnetic disks and tapes. Other components used are magnetic bubble memory and optical disks. Auxiliary storage is usually organised in records or blocks.

Section 2

Types of memory

This section details the physical implementation of various memory devices whose logical properties and uses were presented in Section 1.

Semiconductor memories

Semiconductor memory devices are chips just like the microprocessor. Depending on the desired overall size of the computer system memory, there may be just a few or many such chips.

The uses of the two classes of semiconductor memory introduced in Chapter 3 are discussed below.

RAM

Computers almost invariably use RAMs for their high speed main memory (and use slower speed memories to hold auxiliary data). RAM is used for storing programs and data that are subject to change and their content is lost at power switch off.

RAM devices can be further classified into:

- static RAM (SRAM), generally used for cache systems;
- dynamic RAM (DRAM), generally used for main memory systems.

SRAM consists essentially of internal flip-flops that store the binary information, with the information remaining available as long as power is applied to the unit. DRAM stores the binary information in the form of electric charges and needs to be refreshed every few milliseconds. It has larger storage capacity per chip, but SRAM has shorter Read/Write cycles and needs less additional hardware to support the memory chips.

Read only memory (ROM)

ROM memories are of random access type, with the difference that they store data, once written, permanently, and cannot be written to by the computer in which they are installed.

ROMs are used for storing programs that are permanently resident in the computer and other data that does not change value during its normal use. A typical usage for ROM is that of the 'bootstrap loader' or BIOS (basic input/output system), an initial program, run when the computer power is switched on. The bootstrap loader brings a portion of the operating system from disk to the main memory, gives control to the operating system and prepares the computer for general use.

The hardware interface to a ROM is similar to that for a RAM although, obviously, there is no WRITE input (although for a 'programmable ROM' there may be a 'PROGRAM' input). Several types of ROMs are currently available:

- Mask-programmed ROMs: used when a large number of ROM units containing a particular program or data is required. The program or data is 'burned' into the unit. This ROM is custom fabricated to suit a particular application.
- User-programmed ROMs (PROMs): a PROM programmer is used to 'burn' the required program into the chip. Most PROMs can be erased if required for re-use, either by using ultra-violet light or an electrical signal.

Section 3

Auxiliary storage devices

This section introduces the different kinds of auxiliary storage device, how they work and what they're used for.

Interfacing storage devices

Storage devices need to transfer large amounts of data to and from the computer quickly. For this reason they use parallel interfaces and block DMA transfer of data (see Chapter 6 for an explanation of this). There are two common interface standards in use currently, the integrated device electronics (IDE) interface, otherwise known as ATA, and the small computer systems interface (SCSI), which allows the use of more and varied types of device, and tends to be used for larger computers and servers.

Storage devices use one of two storage methods, magnetic or optical, or occasionally a combination of both.

CRUCIAL CONCEPT

Optical recording uses laser light beams to record a series of dots encoding the data to be recorded, or pits in the recording medium. The dots can be read using a laser to track the trail of dots. If a photocell is used to record the density of light reflected off the medium the current from the cell will vary according to whether there is a dot or not, causing a signal that can be decoded to restore the original data.

The dots or pits can be generated in different ways. They can be pressed into the medium using a 'stamper' (obviously this can only be done at a factory), or the medium may contain a dye that changes colour when heated by a scanning laser, or it may contain a thin layer of some substance that can be 'burned' or 'bubbled' by the laser. In the latter case, a second application of the laser might smooth it out again, allowing the medium to be reused.

Optical recording can achieve high densities and is robust, but tends to be slow.

CRUCIAL CONCEPT

Magnetic recording media are coated with a material that can be magnetised. A small electromagnet, known as a recording head, can magnetise this material, using alternating magnetisation polarities to encode a data pattern. It is inherently reusable.

When such a magnetised pattern is moved under a similar head, it will induce in it an electrical current which can be used to reconstruct the data. Another technique is to use opto-magnetic recording. Here, the magnetic material is only active if exposed to light. A laser beam is used to activate a region much smaller than the head itself, allowing more data to be recorded. Magneto-optical effects (substances whose reflectivity depends on magnetic fields) can be used to allow reading of data at a high density.

Magnetic recording can be very fast, but is not very robust. High recording densities rely on scrupulous exclusion of dust and foreign particles. Magneto-optical recording can be more robust than straightforward magnetic recording

Disks

Disks and tapes are the most common auxiliary memory devices used in computer systems.

Magnetic disks

Magnetic disk memory provides large storage capabilities and moderate operating speed. They store information on one or more circular **platters** coated with magnetic material. The plates are continuously spinning (with speeds from 5400 to 10000 RPM) and are stacked on a spindle, with space between them. Tracks are divided into sectors. Commonly there is a single Read/Write head for each disk surface mounted on a common arm. This head needs to be placed accurately and quickly on the selected track.

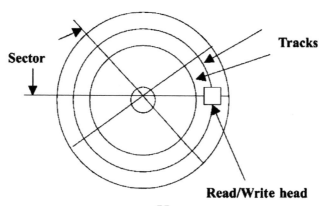

Tracks

Sector

Read/Write head

A disk system is addressed by address bits that specify the disk number, the disk surface, the sector number and the track within the sector. After the Read/Write heads are positioned in the specified track, the system has to wait until the rotating disk reaches the specified sector under the head. Once the beginning of a sector has been reached, information transfer is fast.

- Hard disks: the usual device is what is known as a 'Winchester disk'. The medium is built in as an integral part of the disk and is not removable, allowing it to be sealed at manufacture with an extremely clean, controlled atmosphere, which means very small heads can be used and data packing density can be very high. Standard disk diameters are 3.5 inches for desktop machines and 2.5 inches for portable computers. Capacities may range from a few gigabytes (billion bytes) to hundreds of gigabytes.
- Floppy disks: a flexible plastic disk in a plastic sleeve. Capacity of floppy disks is small (1.4 Mbytes typically), so they are really restricted to data transfer from one machine to another, and are becoming less useful for that as data sizes become larger. 'Floptical' disks, which are similar but use a laser beam to locate the head over the surface of the disk, so achieving more accurate positioning and a higher data capacity, have a capacity of 100Mbytes.

Magnetic tape

A magnetic tape is a strip of plastic coated with a magnetic recording medium. Bits are recorded as magnetic spots on tracks (seven or nine). Information is recorded in blocks, called records. There are gaps of unrecorded tape between records, so that the tape can be stopped, started to move forward, or in reverse, or can be rewound. Each record has an identification bit pattern at the beginning (for the tape controls to identify the record number) and at the end (for the controls to recognise the beginning of a gap). A tape is addressed by specifying the record number and the number of characters in the record. With Read/Write heads mounted on each track, data can be read or recorded in the form of whole records. (Note that records can be of fixed or variable length.) Reading is entirely serial.

Tape drives use tape contained in a cartridge for easy loading. Video cassette tape (usually 8mm) or digital audio tape may be used, and there are also several cassette standards specifically for data. Storage capacity will be in the order of several to several hundred Gigabytes.

Optical storage devices

Optical storage devices are used to record and retrieve video, audio and image data as well as text and computer data. They have an extremely high-density recording capability, enabling the storage of several Gbytes of data on a disk. Optical storage devices have a much longer life span (tens of years compared to five years for magnetic devices).

There are several types of optical disks, including the following:

- CD: compact disk, a 120mm disk which stores 650 or 700 Mbytes, most effectively used for pre-recorded optical storage, for archival purposes, and can be obtained as a read-only (CD-ROM), write once (CD-R) or rewritable (CD-RW) recordable variant. Data is organised in sectors, which can be read independently, like a hard disk.
- DVD: digital versatile disk. A more modern relative of the CD, with the difference that DVD tracks are narrower. DVDs are read by a laser beam of a shorter wavelength than that used in CD technology. This allows for smaller indentations, hence increased storage capacity. Data is written in two layers, the outer golden layer being semitransparent, to allow reading of the underlying silver layer. Like the CDs, there are several types of DVDs, incuding DVD-ROM (read only), DVD-R (write once, can hold up to 3.95 Gbytes per side), DVD-RAM (rewritable).

Section 4

End of chapter assessment

Multiple-choice answers

1. Which of the following assertions is true?
   a) the central memory is the computer's backing store
   b) the auxiliary memory is the working memory of the computer system
   c) the auxiliary memory is fast and expensive
   d) the central memory is the working memory of the computer system
   e) the central memory is large and slow

2. Starting with the fastest and smallest capacity components, the memory hierarchy is as follows:
   a) cache memory, virtual memory, registers, main memory, auxiliary memory
   b) registers, cache memory, main memory, virtual memory, auxiliary memory
   c) auxiliary memory, virtual memory, registers, cache memory, main memory
   d) virtual memory, registers, cache memory, auxiliary memory, main memory
   e) registers, main memory, cache memory, virtual memory, auxiliary memory

3. Which of the following statements about the cache memory is true?
   a) it holds the most recently accessed code and data
   b) it is only concerned with the transfer of information between the auxiliary memory and the CPU
   c) it is only concerned with the transfer of information between the I/O processor and the CPU
   d) it serves as the interface with the auxiliary memory
   e) it is used to give the appearance of a large memory

4. Which of the following statements about the auxiliary memory is true?
   a) it holds the programs and data currently used by the CPU
   b) the CPU has direct access to the auxiliary memory
   c) the auxiliary memory is very fast
   d) the auxiliary memory is volatile
   e) it holds those parts of programs and data that are not currently used by the CPU

5. What are the primary advantages of SRAM over DRAM?
   a) SRAM has lower power consumption and larger storage capacity
   b) SRAM is volatile and expensive
   c) SRAM is easier to use, has shorter Read/Write cycles and doesn't need any additional hardware
   d) SRAM is easier to use, has longer Read/Write cycles and doesn't need any additional hardware
   e) SRAM needs to be refreshed often

6. ROM memories:
   a) store results of ALU operations
   b) do not hold their content at power switch off
   c) hold their content at power switch off
   d) are of Read/Write random access type
   e) are internally sequential logic devices

7. Magnetic disk memory provides:
    a) fast operating speed
    b) moderate operating speed
    c) slow operating speed
    d) operating speed as slow as the register type memory
    e) operating speed as fast as the cache memory

8. IDE stands for:
    a) interface for disk equipment
    b) internal disk equipment
    c) integrated disk equipment
    d) integrated delivery element
    e) integrated device electronics

9. A computer memory uses RAM chips of 512x1 capacity. How many chips are needed to provide a memory capacity of 1024 bytes?
    a) 8
    b) 16
    c) 2
    d) 24
    e) 32

10. A computer employs RAM chips of 256x8 and ROM chips of 1024x8. The computer needs 2K bytes of RAM and 4K bytes of ROM. What is the total number of chips needed?
    a) 12
    b) 8
    c) 24
    d) 16
    e) 6

11. Which one of these is a commonly available bulk storage technology?
    a) magnetic
    b) holographic
    c) molecular
    d) bionic
    e) quantum

12. Which recording technology does a DVD use?
    a) quantum
    b) holographic
    c) magnetic
    d) magneto-optical
    e) optical

13. What are the recording and replay devices in a hard disk called?
    a) sensors
    b) arms
    c) coils
    d) heads
    e) lasers

Multiple-choice answers

1-d, 2-b, 3-a, 4-e, 5-c, 6-c, 7-b, 8-e, 9-b, 10-a, 11-a, 12-e, 13-d.

Chapter 5
Performance

Chapter summary

This chapter examines how the design of a processor and the surrounding system affects performance, introduces some basic measures of performance and discusses their meaning and limitations.

Learning outcomes

After studying this chapter you should aim to test your achievement of these outcomes by answering the multiple-choice questions and the examples at the end of the chapter. You should be able to:

Outcome 1: Describe the parameters which factor the performance of a computer and explain the limitations on processing speed improvement associated with each factor.

Outcome 2: Describe the constraints on processors achieving their potential speed, the measures that may be taken to over-come these constraints and be able to select which are appropriate to which situations.

Outcome 3: Describe several different measures of processor speed, and select which measure is applicable to different applications.

Outcome 4: Understand the nature of benchmarking, and select bench-marks suitable for predicting performance with different applications.

How will you be assessed on this?

Your understanding might be tested by seeing if you can select the appropriate type of 'speed' for different applications and whether you are able to calculate the instruction execution rate of a given simple processor. The ability to comprehend a manufacturer's specification and compare different products also provides the basis for assessment. Likewise, you will be tested on your knowledge and ability to interpret figures and your ability to estimate the required bandwidths in a system and use the calculations to find bottlenecks.

Useful information sources

Cragon, Harvey G. (1996) *Memory Systems and Pipelined Processors,* Jones and Bartlett, Boston, MA, ISBN 0-86720-474-5 (Chapters 5 and 6).

Mahapatra, R. Nihar, Venkatrao, Balakrishna (2001), *The Processor-Memory Bottleneck: Problems and Solutions,* www.acm.org/crossroads/xrds5-3/pmgap.html

Semiconductors technical sites:
http://developer.intel.com
http://www.amd.com/us-en/Processors/ProductInformation/
http://www.transmeta.com/

(Section 1)

Factors affecting performance

There are several different elements which together contribute to the 'speed' of a computer. This section tells you what they are, and how they are interrelated.

What is the speed of a computer?

Computers are used for a whole variety of purposes, and some measures of speed suit some applications more than others.

Taking a computer as a whole, we can judge the 'performance' in four different aspects.

- Processor performance – how fast does the computer execute the code in programs?
- Data performance – how fast can the computer process large data sets held in main memory?
- I/O performance – how fast can the computer move data from main memory to peripheral devices?
- Device performance – how fast can the peripheral devices, such as disk drives, provide and consume data?

The first two of these are to do with the design of the processor and its immediate support, the bus interface, the memory management, and the main memory system itself, including any caches.

The determining factor in I/O performance depends on the device and the I/O architecture of the computer. In modern computers this can be highly complex. A typical modern PC will have at least four separate I/O buses.

- The PCI (peripheral connect interface) bus, which forms the 'standard' I/O connection.
- The AT bus (named after the original IBM AT PC) which is retained to allow old style IBM PC peripherals to work.
- An AGP (advanced graphics port) connector for the screen hardware.
- A USB (universal serial bus) for simple connection of various peripheral devices.

The correct servicing and sequencing of the different devices can make a considerable difference to the speed with which data is fed to the peripheral devices with a particularly big effect on interactive performance. Often such performance is determined by the way the operating system performs, or is individually configured. Computer components from different suppliers constructed using identical hardware can perform quite differently.

(Section 2)

Clock rate and instruction cycles

For a simple computer, the rate of its clock determines the rate of calculations or instruction execution rate and hence the performance of the computer.

───────── CRUCIAL CONCEPT ─────────

The rate of the clock input to the CPU's control unit is the **processor clock rate**.

Unfortunately, it doesn't tell us anything about the actual program execution speed of the processor unless we know what happens at each 'tick' of the processor clock, when the sequencer executes another operation in the CPU. The sequencer issues the signals that latch values into the processor's internal registers, producing an **instruction step**.

Different processor architectures require a different number of steps to produce a complete instruction, and some require a different number of steps to perform different types of instruction. Many early computers used a basic four step instruction (as in Chapter 3):

- Step 1: fetch instruction;
- Step 2: fetch operand;
- Step 3: perform operation;
- Step 4: write result.

Such a computer takes four clock ticks to execute each instruction – the instruction execution rate being one quarter of the clock rate.

CRUCIAL CONCEPT

The number of steps taken to perform an individual instruction gives the number of **clocks per instruction** (or CPI) of the processor. The instruction execution rate indicates how fast a processor executes instructions. It is calculated by dividing the clock rate (in Hertz or Hz) by the CPI for the processor to yield the number of instructions per second (IPS). The normal measure is **MIPS** (million instructions per second).

A processor with very simple instructions may require a lot more of them to implement a given program than one with more complex instructions.

Section 3

Increasing processor performance

This section examines how the design of a processor may be optimised, and the resultant trade-off between different aspects of performance.

Increasing the clock rate

There are two obvious ways to increase the speed of a processor – increase the clock rate or reduce the CPI. The maximum clock rate depends on the amount of time the logic in the processor takes to perform a single instruction step. If it takes 1 µs for the carry to propagate from the least significant bit to the most significant bit of the ALU a clock speed any higher than 1MHz risks yielding incorrect arithmetic results. The maximum possible clock rate is dictated by the slowest step within the instruction. It might be possible to increase the clock rate still further by splitting that step into two.

The simple, four-step processor described earlier has the following minimum times for each step.

- Step 1: fetch instruction 100ns;
- Step 2: fetch operand 180ns;
- Step 3: perform operation 80ns;
- Step 4: write result 100ns.

The fastest feasible clock speed with this processor is given by $1/(180 \times 10^{-9}) = 5.56\text{MHz}$. It executes instructions at a rate of 5.56/4 = 1.39 MIPS.

Suppose we divide step 2 into those two parts, to yield:

- Step 1: fetch instruction 100ns;
- Step 2a: calculate operand address 80ns;
- Step 2b: fetch operand 100ns;
- Step 3: perform operation 80ns;
- Step 4: write result 100ns.

The fastest feasible clock speed is now $1/(100 \times 10^{-9}) = 10$MHz. It executes instructions at a rate of $10/5 = 2$ MIPS, an increase of nearly 50%.

Reducing CPI

If a separate memory port for instruction fetches was provided we could fetch the next instruction while writing the previous result.

- Step 1: fetch operand 180ns;
- Step 2: perform operation 80ns;
- Step 3: write result /fetch next instruction 100ns.

The fastest feasible clock speed is still 5.56MHz, but the execution rate is $5.56/3 = 1.85$ MIPS, a 25% increase.

Decreasing the number of execution steps will lower the CPI, while increasing them will allow a higher clock rate at the cost of a higher CPI. The processor designer's job is to find the optimum mix for a particular architecture and fabrication technology.

Pipelines

There is a possible way out of this compromise, which is to design this processor as a pipeline. Each step is provided with its own section of the processor and feeds results to the next section. A pipeline, for the five-step processor is shown below.

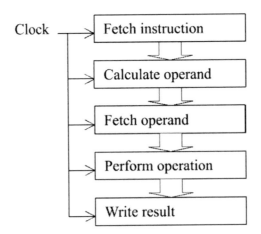

At each clock a new instruction is fetched, an operand address calculated, an operand fetched, an operation performed and a result written. Five instructions are in progress, one in each stage of the pipeline. The following diagram illustrates this.

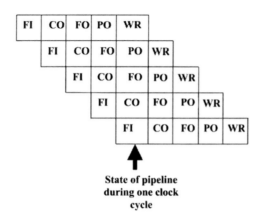

**State of pipeline
during one clock
cycle**

A new instruction is started and completed each clock cycle, so the CPI is 1, giving 10 MIPS, more than a sevenfold increase. The CPI remains 1 however many stages there are in the pipeline, so we can split steps into very small ones if we wish, yielding very high clock speeds and consequently high performance. There are some other factors that will stop us meeting this performance. In each clock cycle the pipeline is performing three memory operations, so requires a memory system three times as fast, or with three separate 'ports'.

When the instruction causes a 'branch', it will modify the address of the next instruction to be executed, available at the end of the instruction, by when the pipeline has already fetched and started the four original instructions. These have to be stopped and the pipeline registers restored before the next instruction can be fetched. This is called 'flushing' the pipeline. Apart from wasting clock cycles, the hardware required is complex, which will tend to slow the operation of the pipeline.

Since each pipeline stage operates every clock cycle, it needs its own dedicated hardware, including a separate ALU in each pipeline stage that performs arithmetic or logical operations.

Finally, the operation of a pipeline assumes that all instructions have the same format and number of steps. Designing a pipeline with enough flexibility for complex instruction sets is difficult.

Reduced instruction set computers

Pipelined processors can be simplified if the instruction set is suitably designed. This might make the instruction set more difficult to program, but since programs are usually produced by a compiler, this is not a problem. This philosophy is classified by the rather misleading term 'reduced instruction set computer' or RISC, after the original developed at the University of California, Berkeley. The name is misleading because most RISC designs have more instructions than CISC (for complex instruction set computer) processors, nor is the 'power' of a RISC instruction significantly different from that of a 'CISC'. RISC design eliminates features of CISC design that makes pipelined operation difficult.

- Variable length instructions and instruction cycles are avoided. Using only a single and double length instruction cycle makes design of the pipeline much simpler, for the reasons outlined above.
- Most operations occur between processor registers and a large complement of registers is provided. This eliminates the need to synchronise with external memory systems and address calculations.
- Load and store instructions are provided to transfer data between memory and processor registers. These are usually 'double length' instructions to allow time for external memory access.

63

- The effect of a branch instruction is delayed until after the instructions in the pipeline have executed, so the pipeline doesn't need to be flushed.

When initially introduced RISC processors outperformed their CISC counterparts because of the speed advantages of a pipeline. Now it is possible to design pipeline implementations of even the most complex CISC machines, and the RISC performance advantage has disappeared. Their simplicity makes them suitable where cost and power consumption are at a premium.

The CPI of a well designed RISC or pipeline CISC processor is higher than 1 due to the double length instructions and the wasted instructions after a branch. Values in the range 1.25-1.5 are common.

Superscalar processors

Imagine we build a processor with two pipelines, as shown below.

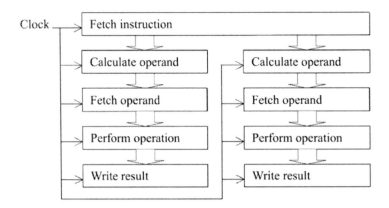

Such an arrangement is called a **superscalar processor**. Each clock cycle, this processor can process two instructions, so long as the 'fetch instruction' stage can fetch two instructions at once, reducing the CPI by half. It is unlikely that this performance will be realised. Frequently an instruction uses a result calculated by a previous one, so it cannot be executed at the same time. A superscalar processor has circuitry which detects dependencies and delays execution of instructions accordingly. Sometimes one pipeline will be unused, reducing the advantage.

Superscalar processors can be designed with more than two pipelines, and individual pipelines might be specialised for different instruction types, but as the number of pipelines increase the speedup diminishes, due to the dependencies. Sophisticated instruction scheduling circuitry can re-order instructions and unoccupied pipelines are used to 'speculatively execute' code following both routes from a branch, allowing uninterrupted processing whatever the result of the branch.

The role of the compiler

CRUCIAL CONCEPT

Most programs are written in high level languages such as C or Java and translated to machine instructions by a program called a **compiler**.

When measuring the performance of a program the compiler itself is within the performance loop. Furthermore, compilers may be used to complement the architectural design of a computer. 'Traditional' compilers were designed around an 'execution stack', an area of memory which contains, among other things, the local variables for a procedure. RISC processors would have taken three instructions for each stack access (a 'load', 'operate' and 'store'). Part of the RISC 'architecture' was a new sort of compiler that used processor registers for local variables instead of the stack, avoiding the problem. In this sense the compiler is a part of the 'architecture' of a processor.

If the compiler generates instructions in small groups which are not interdependent then a superscalar processor will be able to keep its pipelines full. This will have the greatest effect when the compiler has information about the processor.

Taking this idea to its extreme, the compiler could take on the role of ensuring that there are no interdependencies between concurrently executing instructions, issuing 'packets' of instructions, one for each pipeline within the processor. This is called a **very-long instruction word** (VLIW) computer. It can achieve a greater degree of parallelism, and therefore a lower CPI, than a superscalar processor. The work of the complex scheduler is done by the compiler, potentially increasing clock rates. Two examples of VLIW processors are the Intel IA64 and the Trasmeta 'Crusoe' PC.

Section 4

MIPS and FLOPS

MIPS (million instructions per second) and FLOPS (floating point operations per second) are widely used measures of processor speed. This section discusses what they mean and how to interpret MIPS and FLOPS figures.

The MIPS measure of performance

Despite the shortcomings discussed above 'MIPS' has become a commonly used measure of performance. It depends on a commonly agreed performance which represents 1 MIPS and gives a 'benchmark' against which the performance of other computers can be measured. One such is a comparison with the speed of the Digital Equipment Coporation (now Compaq Corporation) VAX11/780 computer, which was a popular '1 MIPS' computer. Often 'MIPS' performance ratings are quoted as 'VAX MIPS'.

For mathematical computation, the key benchmark is performance when calculating using floating point representation of numbers. The performance of all operations between floating point quantities involves both adding and multiplication, so performance can be simply judged, in terms of the number of floating point operations performed.

--- CRUCIAL CONCEPT ---

FLOPS stands for 'floating point operations per second' and is a measure of the number of floating point operations performed per second by a computer.

Floating point performance is important for graphics and image processing. It is important when judging FLOPS performance to know the length of the floating point variables being used, whether 32-bit (single precision), 64-bit (double precision) and 80-bit (extended precision) versions.

Section 5

Bandwidth and bottlenecks

To perform well all parts of the computer must be fast enough to support the others. This section discusses where the bottlenecks are, and how they could be avoided.

CRUCIAL CONCEPT

The **bandwidth** as related to computer subsystems is the rate at which that subsystem needs to transfer data if it is to run at full speed.

Below is a simple bandwidth calculation for two of the processors we have looked at above, making the following assumptions:

- a 32-bit (4 byte) instruction word;
- 20% of instructions executed transfer data to and from memory.

The four cycle processor

This has an instruction throughput of 1.39MIPS, so the memory bandwidth used is:

$1.39 \times 4 \times 8$ million bits per second for instructions $=$ 44.5 million bits per second
$1.39 \times 4 \times 8 \div 5$ million bits per second for data $\quad=$ 8.9 million bits per second

Total bandwidth $\qquad = $ 53.4 million bits per second

If we couple this processor with a 32-bit wide memory system the memory cycle time needs to be:

$32 \div 53\ 400\ 000$ seconds $\qquad = $ 600 nanoseconds

The superscalar processor

This has an instruction throughput of 16 MIPS, so the memory bandwidth used is:

$16 \times 4 \times 8$ million bits per second for instructions $\quad=$ 512 million bits per second
$16 \times 4 \times 8 \div 5$ million bits per second for data $\qquad=$ 102 million bits per second

Total bandwidth $\qquad = $ 614 million bits per second

If we couple this processor with a 32-bit wide memory system the memory cycle time needs to be:

$32 \div 614\ 000\ 000$ seconds $\qquad = $ 52 nanoseconds

One way of doubling the memory bandwidth available is to increase the 'width' of the memory. In practice faster memory is required than is indicated by these simple calculations.

Caches

Subcircuits on the chip can be accessed much faster than those off-chip. The processor can run much faster than the off-chip memory can provide data. The solution is a 'cache', as discussed in the last chapter.

This cache is organised as an array of 'entries' or 'lines'. As well as the data the entry contains a record of the main memory (or sometimes virtual memory) address where the data comes from in a section called the 'tag'. As data is read from memory by the processor, the cache saves it. As the processor makes requests for memory data the address is compared with the tags. If there is a match then that data is provided from the cache, rather than main memory. Thus the cache can speed up accesses to memory locations that have been recently used.

The design of a cache affects the 'hit ratio' of the cache, which affects the required memory bandwidth, as in the following example.

If the superscalar processor is interfaced to the main memory system via a cache with an 80% hit ratio, then one-fifth of memory accesses are passed on to memory, so the memory bandwidth required is now:

$$614\ 000\ 000 \times 1/5 = 122.8 \text{ million bits per second}$$

The cache has reduced the memory bandwidth by five. Sometimes caches can be 'flushed', typically by a program which reads a very large data structure from one end to the other. If this happens the processor will run at one fifth of the speed, limited by the memory bandwidth. Attention to the design of the inner loops of programs can have a large effect on the performance of cached processors.

Section 6

End of chapter assessment

Questions

1. Using the 'four step' processor example given in Section 3, what would be the performance of a design that both split step 2 and merged the instruction fetch step with the write result step?
2. What would be the effect on performance of the original four-step processor of splitting step 3, perform operation, into two steps, each taking 40ns?
3. What would be the performance in MIPS of the original four-step processor if redesigned as a pipeline?
4. What is the memory bandwidth required for the processor described in example 3, assuming a 16-bit instruction word and one 32-bit data transfer every ten instructions?
5. Given a 32-bit memory system, what is the memory cycle time?
6. What would it be if interfaced via a cache with a 70% hit rate?

Answers

1. Steps are now:

Step 1: calculate operand address	80ns;
Step 2: fetch operand	100ns;
Step 3: perform operation	80ns;
Step 4: write result/fetch next instruction	100ns.

   Maximum clock rate is 10MHz, execution rate is 10/4 = 2.5 MIPS, an increase of nearly 80% over the original.

2. Steps are now:

Step 1: fetch instruction	100ns;
Step 2: fetch operand	180ns;
Step 3a: perform operation 1	40ns;
Step 3a: perform operation 2	40ns;
Step 4: write result	100ns.

   The fastest feasible clock speed with this processor is given by $1/(180 \cdot 10^{-9}) = 5.56$MHz. It executes instructions at a rate of $5.56/5 = 1.112$ MIPS, a decrease of 20%.

3. Pipeline is as shown:

   Slowest stage = 180ns, clock rate = 5.56MHz
   Instruction execution rate = 5.56MIPS

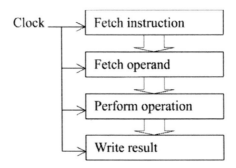

4. Instructions = 5 560 000 × 16 = 88 960 000 bits/second
   Data = 5 560 000 × 32/10 = 17 792 000 bits/second
   Total = 106 752 000 bits/second

5. 32/(106 752 000) = 299ns

6. Total memory rate = 106 752 000 × 3/10 = 32 025 600 bits/s
   Cycle time = 32/(32 025 600) = 1 microsecond.

Multiple-choice questions

1. Which of these is not an aspect of a computer's performance?
   a) device
   b) processor
   c) brand
   d) I/O
   e) data

2. Which of these is not a type of I/O bus?
   a) AT
   b) MP
   c) AGP
   d) USB
   e) PCI

3. Which word describes the fact that a computer performs calculations on the 'ticking' of a clock?
   a) psychotic
   b) syncopated
   c) synonymous
   d) synchronised
   e) simplified

4. What is an instruction cycle?
   a) the sequence of instructions in a program loop
   b) re-use of instruction cache memory
   c) a two-wheeled robot conveyance
   d) the sequence of steps required to make a complete instruction
   e) a set of computer instructions which do nearly the same thing

5. What does the abbreviation MIPS stand for?
   a) millions of instructions per second
   b) million instruction program schedule
   c) multi inheritance program style
   d) multiple issue processor sequencer
   e) multiple input processor stream

6. If a processor has a six-step instruction cycle with the longest step being 10ns, what is the highest possible clock rate?
   a) 60MHz
   b) 166MHz
   c) 16.66MHz
   d) 600MHz
   e) 100MHz

7. Which of these will not increase the performance of a processor?
   a) increase clock rate
   b) reduce clocks per instruction
   c) fit a larger heatsink
   d) design a pipelined processor
   e) design a superscalar processor

8. How many instructions per clock cycle does a single pipelined processor process?
   a) 1
   b) 1/2
   c) 2
   d) as many as there are stages in the pipeline
   e) 10

9. What is a superscalar processor?
   a) a very large processor
   b) a very small processor
   c) a processor with multiple pipelines
   d) a special purpose co-processor
   e) a top of the range processor

10. What is the effect of a cache?
    a) doubles the speed of a processor
    b) reduces the cost of a processor
    c) increases clock rate of a processor
    d) reduces cycle time of a processor
    e) reduces the number of memory accesses made by a processor

Multiple-choice answers

1-c, 2-b, 3-d, 4-d, 5-a, 6-e, 7-c, 8-a, 9-c, 10-e.

Chapter 6
Peripherals

Chapter summary

We have seen the notion of 'peripheral device' earlier in this book. This chapter introduces the different types of peripherals, what they do and their characteristics.

Learning outcomes

After studying this chapter you should aim to test your achievement by answering the multiple-choice questions at the end of the chapter. You should be able to do the following things.

Outcome 1: Describe the difference between character, block and raster devices and classify different devices into these categories.

Outcome 2: Describe parallel and serial methods of interfacing a device to a computer bus, and discuss which method is suitable for a particular device.

Outcome 3: Enumerate a number of different types of peripheral device, describe what they are for and have an overview of how they are interfaced to a computer.

How will you be assessed on this?

You should have the ability to select appropriately between peripherals for different roles, to understand what tasks different peripheral devices are capable of and the demands a peripheral is likely to make on the computer hardware and software. It is this ability which is likely to be tested. You should also know the most likely interfacing method for a particular type of device, and the effects that this has on its performance and program interface.

You need to know what types of display device there are, have an overview of how they work and what they are good for. It is also worthwhile knowing how a printer works so that you can make suitable selections for different applications. This can be assessed by presenting you with scenarios and asking you to make appropriate choices.

Useful information sources

PC Tech Guide, http://www.pctechguide.com

Section 1

Types of peripheral

Here we look at the different broad types of peripheral device.

Classifying peripherals

One way of classifying peripherals is by what *they do*. The other way is according to the way *the computer interfaces with them*. In this section we classify peripherals by the way the computer interfaces with them into **character**, **block** and **raster** devices and whether it is an **input device**, an **output device** or an **input/output device**. Usually the hardware interface to a device is two way (input and output), whether or not the device is input or output only.

CRUCIAL CONCEPT

In a **character device** data is transferred in small, individual units, usually of eight bits and often containing a code representing an alpha-numeric character. The most commonly used coding system is called ASCII, which is often used for internal data storage of character information as well. Sometimes the data transferred represents some other code. Whether or not the information refers to a character, we shall call any device that transfers data in small individual units a character device. Some peripherals use or provide data in larger units, maybe of some hundreds or thousands of bytes at a time, maybe to handle data at a high speed. These are called **block devices**. A **raster device** is like a two-dimensional block, used to represent a two-dimensional graphics. Raster devices are devices which produce or accept data organised as a raster.

Section 2

Interfacing peripherals

This section introduces the different ways that peripheral devices are connected to the host computer.

Parallel devices

From the computer's point of view peripherals appear as a register or set of registers on the bus. In hardware terms this simply means that there is a register attached to the bus and an address decoder which clocks data into/out of the register. The inputs or outputs of this register on the 'far side' of the bus directly provide a byte or more of data to the interfaced device. Devices directly connected to a register like this are known as *parallel* devices.

Serial devices

One problem with a parallel interface is that it requires several wires to connect. As data speeds increase, the 'skew' between different individual signal wires can become significant. One way round this is to interface the device **serially** using a **shift register**. After each byte of data is loaded, the shift register is clocked, once for each bit, causing the bits to appear sequentially at the output, which is connected by a single wire to a receiving shift register. This is clocked at the same rate, causing the bits of the data to be reassembled into a parallel form.

A generic serial interface for data transmission is shown below.

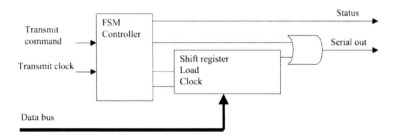

The finite state machine receives a transmit command and produces the following sequence:

- a character or byte is loaded into the shift register;
- sufficient clock signals to the register are generated to shift the character out on the serial out line;
- the status line is asserted to signal that the interface is ready to transmit another character.

The receiver is similar, except that a serial to parallel shift register is used to shift data in from a serial input, and the sequence is reversed. Both transmitter and receiver must be clocked at the same rate. If they have independent clock generators (known as asynchronous transmission) then they can be synchronised only for a short period of time. To enable the clock generator to be started at the right time the character is prefixed by a **start bit**, and ends with one or two **stop bits** (the OR gate in the serial output path allows the FSM to generate these). In synchronous transmission the receive clock is generated from the transmit clock and guaranteed to be synchronised, start and stop bits are not required.

The transmitter and receiver, along with a clock generator and buffer registers on the data bus, are usually packaged together in a device called a UART (universal asynchronous receiver/transmitter) or a USART (universal synchronous/asynchronous receiver/transmitter).

Register and memory interfaced devices

Some devices are organised as an array of registers, and can be accessed using memory read and write operations. This memory might appear to be 'read-only' (for an input device), or 'write-only' for an output device.

A DMA device has its own dedicated processor (sometimes shared) which can take the system bus over from the main processor and transfer data directly from memory to the device registers. DMA is usually used for devices requiring a high data throughput.

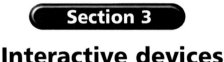

Interactive devices

Interactive devices are the devices people use to give and receive information to the computer. This section introduces them.

Keyboards

A keyboard is usually the major means by which the user enters information and commands to the computer. The keys usually follow the layout of a typewriter, known as 'Qwerty', after the first five keys of the alpha part of the keyboard. A keyboard will usually have a number of additional keys. Each key has a switch placed underneath it, connected together in rows and columns. A keypress connects a row to a column. The columns are 'scanned' using a small microprocessor, driving each high in turn. When connected the output of that row is high when the column is scanned and the corresponding code is sent. PC keyboards send a code when a key is pressed and when it is released, allowing the software to detect 'chords'.

Mice and pointing devices

The mouse is a small box with one to three buttons. As the mouse moves over a surface the movement is detected, using a ball which rolls over the mouse mat. This movement is captured by two rollers placed at right angles to each other and read using an optical encoder. Data identifying the direction of movement and which button has been pressed is sent to the computer using a serial connection.

- A **trackerball**, is simply an upside-down mouse, with a larger ball that can be moved directly with the fingers.
- An **eraserhead** (for laptops) is a small rubber-headed button in the middle of the keyboard. The button has force sensors which detect pressure in the two directions. Movement events are issued at a rate proportional to the pressure applied.
- A **touch panel** is a small panel which can detect the presence and position of a fingertip placed on its surface, using an scanning technique with row and column wires connected resistively or capacitively. Alternatively, the panel may measure the pressure at the four corners of the panel and calculate the position from the relative pressures.

Mouse-type devices produce movement events only. The touch panel is capable of sensing absolute position. If a touch panel is made large it becomes a **tablet**, an absolute position pointing device. Tablets are usually operated with a pen or a **puck** (a small mouse-like device). They can be made transparent and overlayed directly over the screen (called a **touchscreen**).

Sound

Sound is produced by pressure waves in the air, and these are converted to electrical signals by transducers – loudspeakers (signals to sound) and microphones (sound to signals). The sound system of a personal computer usually allows for two sound **channels**, one for each ear. Sound signals are **analogue** signals, the voltage varies with the strength of the sound pressure. The computer converts this to a series of numbers which represent the strength, a **digital** signal, using an **analogue to digital converter** or **ADC** (for sound input) or a **digital to analogue converter** or **DAC** (for sound output). To convert faithfully the analogue signal level must be sampled at a rate of at least twice the highest frequency to be reproduced, at least 32 thousand samples per second.

Good fidelity is gained using a 16-bit sample, which provides 2 bytes of data for each sample. Thus the data rate required for each channel is 32000 x 2 bytes per second, making 128 000 bytes per second. A computer sound system will handle 44100 samples per second at 16 bits per sample per channel (the compact disk rate), down to 8000 samples per second at 8 bits per sample (telephone rate). The data must be supplied continuously, so sound cards will use direct memory access (DMA), and are block devices, both for input and output.

Section 4

Displays

The display is the most visible part of a computer's user interface. Here we meet the different types of display and learn about their characteristics.

The CRT display

The display, or screen, is the central mechanism by which the computer presents information to the user. The interface between the computer and the display is based around the requirements of the **cathode ray tube (CRT)**. The image is provided by **scanning** a very small, bright spot of light across the screen, so quickly that it appears to be a continuous sheet of light. The spot scans across to form a **line** of the image, then 'flies back' to scan the next line, repeating until the screen has been covered. As the spot is scanned its brightness is varied using a **video signal**.

A colour CRT uses three dots, and three corresponding video signals, one for each of red, blue and green.

The video driver hardware divides each scan line into an equal number of **pixels** (short for picture elements), the brightness and colour of each being encoded to a number, which are placed in a shift register and clocked out to provide the pixels within each scan line. This is fed to a RAMDAC (combination of random access memory and digital to analogue converter), which converts it into an analogue RGB signal and sends it over the video cable to the monitor, using a look-up table (the RAM) to convert the digital signal to a voltage level for each colour. There is one digital-to-analogue converter (the DAC) for each of the primary colours used.

CRUCIAL CONCEPT

The number of pixels displayed on the screen is called the **display resolution**, usually measured as $x \times y$, where x is the number of pixels across the screen and y is the number vertically.

Typical screen sizes (in pixels) might range from VGA (video graphics array), 480 lines of 640 pixels, to specialist graphics adaptors with 1280 lines of 1664 pixels.

The number of colours that can be displayed depends on the RAMDAC hardware and may range from 8 bits (256 different colours) to 32 bits (4294967296 colours).

CRUCIAL CONCEPT

The other parameter that affects the specification of the display is the **refresh rate**, how often the complete screen is retraced.

If the refresh rate is too slow the user can see the screen flicker, which can be annoying and tiring. At a refresh rate of 50Hz many people will perceive flicker, at 75Hz few will.

A VGA screen, using 8-bit pixels and refreshed at 50Hz, will require an average data rate of $307200 \times 1 \times 50$ bytes/second = 15 360 000 bytes/second (actually the peak rate is higher than this by maybe 25%, since the spot takes time to 'fly back').

A 1280 × 1664 pixel screen, using 32-bit pixels and refreshed at 75Hz, will require 638 976 000 bytes/second.

Continuous DMA access of memory at that rate by the display system would slow down the main processor, so the display system has its own dedicated display memory, which may be of a specialised memory type such as VRAM (Video RAM) or WRAM (Windows RAM).

The image on the screen is modified simply by modifying the contents of the display memory. Most display adapters have a special purpose processor designed to perform the required operations very quickly. Extra display memory is often available for caching information for the graphics processor.

Using a graphics processor the CPU sends drawing instructions to the card's on-board processor, which can handle these tasks in hardware at far greater speeds than software.

The LCD display

The most popular alternative is the **liquid crystal display** (**LCD**), which is flat and very compact. Liquid crystals modify the polarisation of light when placed in an electric field. An LCD consists of a glass sandwich, with crossed polarisers so that no light can pass through, and contain liquid crystal. The glasses are coated with transparent electrodes in a rectangular array. When a voltage is applied between pixels the liquid crystal 'twists' the polarisation, allowing light to pass through. A flat lamp behind the display generates the light and pixels are filtered red, green and blue to give a coloured display.

Thin film transistor (TFT) switches at the site of every pixel control the pixel voltages, and these are scanned to switch the voltage to the appropriate pixel at the right moment. When the switch is opened again, the pixel remains charged, so a TFT LCD does not flicker.

It is difficult to manufacture a perfect LCD, so they tend to be expensive and the maximum size is more limited.

The plasma display

A plasma display is a flat panel that can be manufactured in larger sizes. Two sheets of glass, printed with electrode patterns, sandwich another sheet pierced with an array of holes, one for each pixel and filled with a gas at low pressure. When a high voltage is placed across the electrodes the gas ionises, producing a plasma, which emits light.

The inside surface of each pixel is coated with a **phosphor**, which absorbs light of one colour and emits light of another. Plasma panels are very expensive, due both to the cost of fabrication and the high voltage electronics required to drive the pixel array.

Section 5

Printers

Printers provide a means of producing 'hard copy' from a computer. Here we look at printer technology.

Types of printer

There are two types of printer: character printers, which print a fixed range of alphanumeric characters, and raster printers, which print a pattern of pixels on the paper. Most printers are raster printers. The quality of a raster printer is measured by the number of dots it prints on the paper; 300 dots per inch (DPI) is the minimum for good quality print.

Rasters to be printed are encoded into characters using a **printer control language**, two common ones being PostScript and Hewlett-Packard Printer Control Language (HPCL). The characters may be sent via a parallel interface, known as a 'centronics' interface or 'PC printer port', or 'serial'.

The printer is equipped with a **raster image processor** (**RIP**), which converts the printer control language description of the page to pixel data. The hardware itself is usually an **ink-jet** or a **laser** printer 'engine'.

Ink-jet printers

The print image is built up from ink drops ejected from a print head which traverses the paper. After each traverse the print carriage moves the paper so that the head can print another 'stripe'.

The head consists of an ink tank connected to print nozzles. These are too small for ink to flow on its own, it needs to be squirted out, either with a tiny electric heater, creating a bubble of steam, or tiny 'piezoelecric' pumps. Colour printers replicate the printhead for black and the three 'subtractive' primary colours: yellow, cyan and magenta.

Modern ink-jet printers produce very high quality images of near photographic quality. They are not suitable for high volume printing.

The laser printer

A laser is modulated by a video signal to scan a pattern of dots onto a photosensitive cylinder. The dots on the cylinder are electrically charged and attract very fine grains of 'toner', a coloured wax. When a sheet of paper is pressed against the cylinder and heated the toner image is transferred to the paper. Laser printers can produce high quality images quickly but are more expensive and larger than ink-jet printers. They are suitable for high throughput applications.

Specialist printers

There are several types of specialist printers including dye sublimation printers, which produce photographic quality images (but expensively), large format inkjet printer/plotters, photoplotters and photosetters for the reprographics industry.

Specialist peripherals

There are types of peripheral that don't fit into the categories we've discussed above. Here they are.

Modems

'Modem' stands for modulator/demodulator and converts a serial logic signal into a form which can be transmitted over some other communications medium. Normal POTS (plain old telephone system) modems have a maximum data speed of 56kbit/second. Broadband

and cable modems have higher bandwidths. Modems connect to the computer via the standard serial interface, some have a UART integrated onto the card.

Scanners

Scanners are used to digitise images for input into computer systems. They work by scanning the image with an array of light sensitive cells, producing a raster representation of the image.

Games controllers

Video games demand a specialist control input, either a joystick or a 'games pad', both similar in operation to the eraserhead, along with a few control buttons. Gamepads are usually interfaced via a special purpose parallel interface, which is often integrated into the sound card. Some gamepads can give 'force feedback' to the user.

TV cards

A TV card may include facilities for digitising video input, encoding video output into a form suitable for display on a standard TV, and a television tuner to convert off-air broadcasts to video for digitising.

Card readers

A card reader reads data off a data card such as a credit card, library card, etc. The data may be encoded on a magnetic strip or it may be contained in a memory chip embedded on the card (usually known as a 'smart card').

Section 7

End of chapter assessment

Multiple-choice questions

1. Which is not a term associated with types of computer peripheral?
   a) character
   b) raster
   c) parallel
   d) serial
   e) chunk

2. What does USART stand for?
   a) universal system archive resource technique
   b) unsynchronised serial access receiver/transmitter
   c) universal synchronous/asynchronous receiver/transmitter
   d) untested systems are really troublesome
   e) unsynchronised sending and receiving technology

3. Which of these devices is an 'interactive' device?
   a) tape drive
   b) keyboard
   c) hard disk
   d) floppy disk
   e) DVD

4. What is the term used for two keyboard keys being pressed simultaneously?
   a) chord
   b) choir
   c) concert
   d) twin
   e) chunk

5. Which of these is not a pointing device?
   a) mouse
   b) eraserhead
   c) touch panel
   d) cursor key
   e) trackerball

6. Which is the main output device on a sound card?
   a) loudspeaker
   b) headphone
   c) DAC
   d) DAT
   e) RAC

7. Which is the most expensive display technology?
   a) CRT
   b) plasma panel
   c) CRT
   d) AGP
   e) VGA

8. Which colour ink would you not expect to find in a colour printer?
   a) red
   b) black
   c) cyan
   d) magenta
   e) yellow

9. Which one of these might be used in a 'smart card' to store its data?
   a) hard disk
   b) memory chip
   c) floppy disk
   d) virtual memory
   e) knotted string

10. Which of these might be found in a games controller?
    a) force feeding
    b) force majeur
    c) force feedback
    d) force feeling
    e) force linking

Multiple-choice answers

1-e, 2-d, 3-b, 4-a, 5-d, 6-c, 7-b, 8-a, 9-b, 10-c.

Chapter 7
Selecting and upgrading systems

Chapter summary

Sometimes it might be necessary to upgrade a computer. This chapter introduces the issues surrounding upgrading and whether it is worthwhile or not.

Learning outcomes

After studying this chapter you should aim to test your achievement by answering the multiple-choice questions and the examples at the end of the chapter. You should be able to do the following things.

Outcome 1: Read and understand computer specifications and make an appropriate choice for a computer for a particular application.

Outcome 2: Understand the cost implications of computer manufacturing technologies, and make appropriate choices based on cost.

Outcome 3: Understand the issues surrounding upgrading, and make appropriate decisions as to whether or not to upgrade.

Outcome 4: Know how to locate which components to upgrade to alleviate a particular problem, and to make that upgrade if necessary.

How will you be assessed on this?

Questions on required performance will be scenario-based, inviting you to make an appropriate analysis of the requirements. With regard to purchasing, can you look at computer specifications and understand their cost implications? Can you make an appropriate decision, given a requirement and a specification? Given the facts, can you make sensible decisions about upgrades? Can you select whether an upgrade or replacement is best?

Useful information sources

E. Watermolen, (1996) *The Basics of Buying a Personal Computer System*, http://www.magicnet.net/~ericwat/buypc.htm

Section 1

Assessing required performance

One of the hardest things to judge is what level of performance is required in a computer system. Knowing the factors that affect performance, and the type of use that a computer is likely to be put to can help you make sensible decisions.

Factors affecting performance

Every major subsystem of a computer can affect its performance, as follows.

- The processor. In 'number crunching' applications processor performance, whether fixed or floating point, is the prime determinant.
- The processor cache. Running at full speed depends on the majority of the program's 'working set' being contained in the cache. The working set of some programs is much larger than others, and such programs will run much faster if the cache is large enough to hold the working set.
- The main memory system. The effect of memory speed depends on the effectiveness of the processor cache, and the speed of the processor with respect to that of the memory.
- The virtual memory system. Modern operating systems use 'virtual memory'. If the main memory is not big enough to hold all the data required immediately for all of the programs running at a time the system is likely to 'thrash', continuously moving data to and from the hard disk.
- The display system. Display performance is one of the main subjective indicators of computer speed, so it is important to get it right.
- The disk system. The extent to which the disk system affects the performance of the computer depends on how much data is being transferred to and from the disk, and how that data is distributed on the disk.
- Other peripherals. Depending on the type of application, specialist peripherals might have an undue affect on the performance of the system.
- The operating system. Reasons for poor performance are often to do with very poor set up of shared resources, such as memory, interrupts, DMA channels or the system registry. A simple reconfigure of the operating system can give huge increases in performance.
- Software. Sometimes a rogue software application can consume system resources, affecting the performance of every other program.

CRUCIAL TIP

Based on the discussion above, when specifying a computer or planning an upgrade the first information needed is: what type of use will the computer be put to? The more information that can be gleaned about this, the better informed the decision will be, but often even an informed guess is better than nothing at all.

The major questions to ask are:

- The requirements of the programs likely to be run. If you know what they are, it is likely that the technical documentation of the programs will give you some indication. You need to check whether the requirements are assessed inclusive or exclusive of the assumed requirement of the operating system. If you don't know you need to make a 'guesstimate'.
- The number of programs likely to be run simultaneously. If you are not to make an overestimate of the amount of memory resource required, you need to know the characteristics of the program and operating system. A given word processor may require 4Mbyte of memory for the program itself. On top of that it may require say 2Mbyte for each separate document that is opened, so if a single instance of the word processor has opened four different documents, the memory requirement is $4+4 \times 2$Mbyte $= 12$Mbyte. If, on the other hand, four separate copies of the word processor are run, each with a single document open, the memory requirement is $4(4+2)$Mbyte, $= 24$Mbyte.
- The number of users. Some systems, typically servers, require to service many users simultaneously. In this case there will be a resource overhead in terms of per user data structure and also cache systems, both memory and disk, will tend to flush rapidly.

Usually this dictates which specialist peripherals need to be included. One way of determining what will be required is to construct a 'use case', a scenario of everyday use of the computer to consider the following:

- Are there the facilities to capture the information that the computer will process? For instance is there a network, a CD drive, camera or scanner, as appropriate to the use of the computer?
- Are there facilities to output the data and allow draft prints as necessary, such as an appropriate printer, networked connection to a network printer, CD writer etc?
- Are there facilities to back up the data? This might be a network connection or a CD or tape drive.

Examples

1. A computer is to be used primarily by a single user for image processing in the reprographics industry. The size of the image to be processed is up to 10000 pixels square, using a full colour 48 bits per pixel representation. The software to be used has many computational filters for image manipulation. What type of computer is required?

   The size of one image is $10000 \times 10000 \times 6$ bytes = 600 Mbyte. Main memory must be large enough to hold one object in its entirety, say 1 Gbyte. The application is computationally intensive, many operations being floating point, so as high a performance processor as is possible would be required. High 3-D graphics performance is not required, so a basic graphics adaptor may be applicable. With 600MByte images, disk storage requirements will be high, however the system will not be required to perform many disk operations simultaneously, so a single disk drive will suffice, if large enough. Backup and a means of inputting and outputting processed images will be required. A CD drive holds 650MByte, so could be used as a means of transfer, but wouldn't be suitable for backup. A writable DVD drive would cover both functions.

2. A computer is to be used as a file server serving 1000 users on a 10Mbit/second Ethernet network. The server will use the Linux operating system.

   Linux is a relatively efficient system. Furthermore, the required performance is limited by the amount of data that can be transferred using a 10Mbit network. Processor performance is not a priority. The display will only be used for system maintenance, so a basic display is OK. The disk system needs to be able to cope with multiple transactions simultaneously, which suggests multiple disk drives for performance rather than capacity. Adequate backup facilities will be required, preferably a high capacity tape.

Section 2

Purchasing decisions

Price and performance are not simply linked. This section introduces the issues of cost and performance to help you make appropriate decisions.

Yield and cost

Semiconductors such as microprocessors and memories are essentially printed onto a 'wafer' of silicon and then split up into the individual 'chips'. The production costs are the production of a wafer, the cost of an individual chip depends on how many can be produced on the wafer, so if a wafer is split into 1000 chips each chip costs 1/1000 the cost of the wafer. The second issue to be considered is called **yield**.

CRUCIAL CONCEPT

Not all chips that are manufactured on a wafer work. The percentage of good ones is called the **yield**.

Every wafer contains imperfections which will stop a chip printed onto that part of the wafer working. If the wafer has N fatal flaws per unit area and the area of an individual chip is A then the probability of a good chip is given by e^{-NA}. If the chip area is 1/N, there is a 50% chance of any chip being good. At 0.7/N almost all of the chips will be good. This chip is half the price, even though it is 0.7 of the size. Conversely if the chip area is 1.3/N almost no good chips will be produced. This chip will be astronomically priced, although only 1/3 bigger. Manufacturers have to balance chip size, yield and cost.

When the chips are made they are tested to see at which speed they will operate successfully, and separated into speed selections, with the higher speed chips being sold for a higher price. Most chips will perform at some optimum speed. As the clock speed is raised the number that will run that fast drops very rapidly, so not many chips will be available at the higher speeds, thus their price will be disproportionately high.

CRUCIAL TIP

To sum this up, at any stage in the development of technology there is an optimum speed or chip size which will be the best value selection. Pushing performance requirements above this point raises performance but at a very high cost. Conversely, there is not much price advantage to be gained by using clock speeds or chip sizes below the optimum.

Volume

Another issue affecting cost is production volume. Standardised PCs are produced in enormous volumes, and there are huge cost advantages in high volume production. Specialist parts are not produced in the same volumes and the economies of scale are smaller, so they can be relatively much more expensive than standard components. One related issue is the cost of outdated components. As volume production is transferred to the latest components, obsolescent components may continue to be produced in smaller volumes for spares, but the cost will be very high.

Section 3

Upgrading

The life of a computer can be extended by upgrading it, sometimes at a lower cost than replacing the machine itself. This section discusses how you decide when you need an upgrade and what upgrading involves.

Is an upgrade necessary?

There is little point upgrading a computer that is operating satisfactorily, so the purpose of an upgrade is to correct a problem. The first thing is to identify the problem correctly. The second issue is whether upgrading is a better option than replacing the computer. Upgrading can be expensive, particularly if the computer is a few years old.

Memory

Additional memory can be one of the most effective ways of increasing the performance of a computer, but only if the performance is limited by a lack of memory.

> ─────────────── CRUCIAL TIP ───────────────
>
> There will usually be two symptoms of a lack of memory. One is 'out of memory' messages, but these really only occur when the situation is very severe. An earlier warning is the signs of the virtual memory system 'thrashing', indicated by continuous hard disk activity even then there is apparently no data being stored or retrieved.

Modern personal computers have a single expandable memory system located on the **motherboard**. Additional memory modules, or **strips**, may be plugged into the memory slots. Before making the upgrade it is necessary to determine how much additional memory is needed and whether slots are available to hold it. If not, it may be necessary to upgrade by replacing of an existing memory strip with one of larger capacity. Your computer or motherboard manual will give precise instructions as to the procedure for adding memory, and also identify the type of strip required.

Disk storage

> ─────────────── CRUCIAL TIP ───────────────
>
> Symptoms of lack of disk space include the obvious running out of space for new files, but also more subtle effects. There needs to be space for virtual memory backing store on the disk. Some operating systems try to allocate this automatically, so it is difficult to tell how much is in use. When it runs out the symptoms are 'out of memory' messages, and unreliability of the operating system.

Most PC motherboards have interfaces for four IDE disk drives. IDE devices generally include hard drives and CD/DVD drives, so in most computers only two are used. If more disk space is required and there is an IDE interface spare, it may be possible simply to add an additional drive. If not it is necessary to replace an existing disk.

The new drive must first be formatted and the contents of the drive to be replaced copied, and the system reassembled with the new drive in place of the old. If the new drive is to be the 'boot' drive (the one to load the operating system on startup) it must be made 'bootable' using an appropriate utility.

Peripherals

Graphic cards use an 'advanced graphics port' (AGP), which comes in a number of speed options, known as 1×, 2× and 4×. The motherboard needs to be able to support the speed option chosen. Some older computers don't have an AGP port, for these an upgraded video card is likely to be expensive.

Other peripherals, such as network cards and modems, only require upgrade if new communications technology becomes available which requires new hardware for support.

Processor

The design of the motherboard will restrict choice to a single range of processors, and on older motherboards the bus interface may not support the highest speed selection of the processor. Due to the limited memory bandwidth available, processor clock rate increases do not deliver a cycle for cycle speed increase. It is quite likely with an elderly motherboard that the memory system will be relatively slow. If this is the bandwidth bottleneck, then a faster processor will not appreciably increase the system speed.

CRUCIAL CONCEPT

In a PC the **motherboard** is the main printed circuit board that connects all the others together. It includes printed circuit 'edge connectors' to take peripheral cards and memory modules. It will also include a connector for a given type of processor, either a socket or a module connector. Motherboards are specific to the type of processor for which they were designed. A motherboard will usually include a number of peripheral interfaces, including disk interfaces, serial and USB ports and parallel printer ports. It may also include video circuitry, sound circuitry and a network interface.

CRUCIAL TIP

The existing memory may be usable with the new motherboard, and all the other peripherals are very likely to be, so the additional cost over that of a processor may be quite small, especially if it enables selection of a processor in the middle of the speed range for that technology (as opposed to the top of an older technology).

Section 4

End of chapter assessment

Questions

1. A computer is to be used as a single user stand alone computer aided design workstation, involving very large data files and realistic 3-D visualisation. When selecting a computer, which components need to be given particular attention and why?

2. A file server is needed as the major data storage for a school. The server will run Linux, and support 50 workstations, mostly running word processing, spreadsheets and Web browsing. Give some outline selection criteria for a suitable computer.

3. The following gives the one-off retail price of a popular processor at different clock speeds. Which one represents the best value in terms of performance per £, and what is the speed ratio between the fastest processor and the best value one?

    1400 MHz £180
    1500 MHz £185
    1600 MHz £190
    1700 MHz £220
    1800 MHz £280
    1900 MHz £350
    2000 MHz £640

Answers

1. There is no 'right' answer, but the application suggests a lot of number crunching, needing a high speed processor. Given the 3-D requirement a high-end 3-D graphics card would be in order, and large memory and disk systems would be required. As a stand-alone system handling expensive data, a secure high volume back-up system (maybe a magnetic tape) would be required.

2. Relatively small data throughput suggests moderate processor requirement. Linux is memory efficient and the number of users small, so very large memory system not is required. Basic display system is required. Network interface will be required. For all servers multiple disks and proper back-up (tape) is required.

3. Best value is 1600MHz at 8.42 MHz/£. The fastest processor is $400 \times 100/1600 = 25\%$ faster.

Multiple-choice questions

1. Which one of these does not directly affect computer performance?
   a) the processor
   b) the power supply
   c) the disk system
   d) the display system
   e) the virtual memory system

2. A semiconductor process gives a yield of 50% with a chip size of 1 square cm. Approximately what would the yield be with a chip size of 2 square cm?
   a) 100%
   b) 75%
   c) 50%
   d) 25%
   e) 0

3. Which of these may be a symptom of memory shortage?
   a) overheating
   b) overeating
   c) continuous display activity
   d) continuous disk activity
   e) hyperactivity

4. Which of these is a popular term for a memory module?
   a) strip
   b) strap
   c) stop
   d) gap
   e) slap

5. Which system is likely to be affected by a lack of disk space?
   a) the processor
   b) the power supply
   c) the disk system
   d) the display system
   e) the virtual memory system

6. Which interface is used to connect hard disks, CDs and DVDs?
   a) AID
   b) RAID
   c) IDE
   d) RIDE
   e) RADE

7. Which interface is used to connect video cards?
   a) GAP
   b) AGP
   c) PAG
   d) GPA
   e) APG

8. With which component does the processor have to be compatible?
   a) the disk drive
   b) the video card
   c) the sound card
   d) the motherboard
   e) the CD drive

9. A bottleneck in which part of the computer may prevent a new processor from achieving its full speed?
   a) the memory
   b) the power supply
   c) the CD
   d) the mouse
   e) the sound card

10. Which interface will not usually be found on a motherboard?
   a) memory module connector
   b) parallel printer port
   c) processor socket
   d) small computer systems interface
   e) universal serial bus

Multiple-choice answers

1-b, 2-e, 3-d, 4-a, 5-e, 6-c, 7-b, 8-d, 9-a, 10-d.

Chapter 8
Basics of operating systems

Chapter summary

The aim of this chapter is to give an overview of operating system concepts, functions and components and how they relate to other components of the computer's architecture. It does not try to explain the internal functioning of an operating system, which would form the subject of a course specifically on operating systems.

Learning outcomes

After studying this chapter you should aim to test your achievement by answering the multiple-choice questions and the examples at the end of the chapter. You should be able to do the following things.

Outcome 1: Explain the meaning of the term 'operating system'.
Outcome 2: List the components of an operating system.
Outcome 3: Explain the function of memory management.
Outcome 4: Explain the role of file systems and the concepts of files, directories and file name space.
Outcome 5: Define what is meant by a 'device' in an operating system context and describe the functions of device management.
Outcome 6: Explain the role of user interface systems and the types in use in modern operating systems.
Outcome 7: Explain the need for and outline the operation of multi-tasking systems.

How will you be assessed on this?

Assessment is likely to be on the basis of your understanding of definitions and facts. The examples here are multiple choice, which is a common way of assessing knowledge of these basic facts.

Examination questions may ask you to show how a specific memory management system would be configured for a specific situation, or to compare the merits of different systems. Practical programming work is also possible.

Filing systems offer a lot of opportunities for practical assessment, such as the correct use of file path names, construction of directory structures for particular purposes and writing programs that use file system parts of the API. Practical examples are also possible with device management, writing programs that use device drivers. Tests and exams will tend to concentrate on your knowledge of the concepts here.

Useful information sources

Patterson, David A. and Hennessy, John L. *Computer Organization and Design: The Hardware/Software Interface*. Morgan Kaufmann, San Francisco. ISBN 1-55860-428-6.
Stallings, W. (2000) *Operating Systems*, Prentice Hall. ISBN: 0-13031-999-6
Tanenbaum, A.S. (2001) *Modern Operating Systems*, Prentice Hall. ISBN 0-13-031358-0

Section 1

What is an operating system?

This section locates the functions of an operating system in the overall architecture of a computer.

The history

Here we look at the major families of operating systems in use today and where they came from.

The Microsoft Windows family of operating systems

The Microsoft operating systems came to commercial attention when their predecessor MS-DOS (standing for Microsoft Disk Operating System) was adopted by IBM for their first PC in 1982. It provided a magnetic disk filing system and a means of loading and running programs from it. In response to the Macintosh system (see below) Microsoft provided the graphical user interface functionality in a new OS layer called MS Windows, that ran as an application over MS-DOS. Later Windows NT (for New Technology) was developed and eventually became Windows 2000. The old, MS-DOS based Windows was continued as Windows 95, Windows 98 and subsequently Windows Me (Millenium edition). The Windows operating systems are by far the most likely to be encountered on PC systems.

The Apple Macintosh operating system

The original Apple Macintosh was the first readily available PC to provide a graphical user interface, in the late 1970s. The Macintosh design was derived from an earlier, less successful, product called Lisa, inspired by Xerox's Star office system, which pioneered the WIMP (windows, icons, menus, pointer) user interfaces.

Unix and Linux

Unix was developed in the early 1970s by Bell Laboratories (part of the American telecommunications company AT&T) as an OS for office computers supporting several users simultaneously. In the 1980s Unix became standard for single user graphical engineering computers. In the early 1990s the rights to Unix were vested in a standards body called X-Open and today Unix is a specification of an API (Applications Programming Interface), and any operating system which conforms can be called Unix, whatever its source. Linux is an 'open source' and free Unix system developed by Linus Thorvalds. Linux runs on standard PCs as well as many other types of computer.

Section 2

Components of an operating system

The view of operating systems structure presented here helps us to understand the structure and purpose of them all.

CRUCIAL TIP

Different operating systems suppliers use different terms for the same thing. Here we have used the generic term, found in most textbooks. Try to spot a software supplier's proprietary term for a well known idea.

Abstraction layers: one view of operating system design is that it is a process of abstraction – replacement of complex detail by a simpler idea that contains the essence without the detail. An operating system abstracts the detail of the computer hardware to leave just the necessary details of the task in the hand.

For instance, to control a serial communications chip may require the use of a number of commands to control the hardware, but all a user program is interested in is sending and receiving characters.

An operating system can be viewed as being constructed from a number of abstraction layers, each one presenting a higher level view of the system functions than the one below it.

If we do this we end up with a picture which looks like a horizontal slice through an onion – hence the onion skin model.

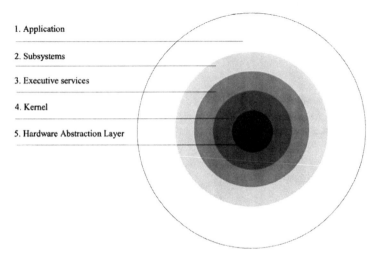

1. Application
2. Subsystems
3. Executive services
4. Kernel
5. Hardware Abstraction Layer

This illustration is of an onion skin model showing the abstraction layers that Microsoft used when they designed the Windows NT operating system.

It's also important not to be misled by the model. The actual software components of an operating system may not be structured in a similar way to the onion skin model. However, the diagram and defined layers make it much easier to understand the function of operating systems.

The functions of the layers in the Windows NT onion skin model are as follows.

1. Applications layer. This layer consists of the applications programs being run by the user.
2. Subsystems layer. This layer provides the applications programming interface (API, see below). In the NT system a number of alternative APIs are maintained.
3. Executive services layer. This layer provides the major operating systems functions such as device drivers, memory management, window management and graphics device interaction.
4. Kernel layer. This is the crucial part of the operating system. It supports the simultaneous running of the programs within the executive services layer which provide the operating systems services.
5. Hardware abstraction layer. This contains all of the processor dependent code, providing a hardware independent interface to the kernel layer.

CRUCIAL CONCEPT

API stands for applications programming interface – a set of operating system instructions, or 'system calls', that a programmer producing an application to run on a given operating system needs to know.

The services provided by most modern operating systems and accessed via the API include:

- memory management;
- file systems;
- process management;
- user interface.

APIs are explained in more detail in Chapters 9 and 10.

Section 3

Memory management

Here we look at the operating system component that ensures that different programs sharing a computer are given access to the memory they need, without interfering with each other.

CRUCIAL CONCEPT

One of the jobs of the operating system is to share the available memory between the different programs. This job is called **memory management**.

Simple memory management consists of two tasks. The first is **memory allocation**, the second **memory mapping**.

Memory allocation is the process whereby the available memory is shared out between the programs. The first program that will require an allocation of memory is the operating system kernel itself, thereafter other programs require to be given memory resources when they are loaded, and sometimes additional resources while they are running. When the program has finished running the memory resources they have used become available for allocation to other programs.

A program needs the following memory resources.

1. The program memory. So far as the program is concerned this is read-only.
2. The data memory. This may be treated as read-only or read/write, depending on the programming environment.
3. The stack memory. The memory required to hold the 'stack' for the program. The stack usually contains return addresses for procedures, parameter values used when calling procedures and local data variables. This is read/write.
4. The 'heap' memory. This is a dynamic memory resource provided by some programming systems. This is read/write.

Often the data and heap memory are included within the stack memory, so a program is represented by two allocations of memory, the program and the stack.

CRUCIAL CONCEPT

One term often used to describe a chunk of memory used for a particular purpose, such as stack or program memory, is **memory segment**.

A segment is often described using two numbers, the **base register**, which gives the start address of the segment and the **limit register**, which gives the highest permissible address usable by that segment. If the memory address is higher than the limit, the instruction is prevented from accessing the memory by the raising of an interrupt or **memory exception**. This prevents inadvertent modification of data in another segment by program errors. Sometimes **base** and **size** registers are used.

The tasks of the memory allocation part of the OS kernel are to:

- keep track of the computer's memory, whether it is **free** or **allocated**;
- allocate and de-allocate memory as it is needed by the programs;
- set up the tables needed by the memory mapping;
- resolve conditions when programs try to access memory outside their own allocated provision;
- rearrange the data stored in the memory to allow optimum use of the system's memory.

CRUCIAL CONCEPT

Logical addresses are the memory addresses as they appear in the program code. **Physical addresses** are the addresses used by the hardware. There is a process of memory-mapping between logical and physical addresses.

The tasks of memory-mapping are to:

- Translate between logical (program) addresses and physical (memory) addresses.
- Detect 'illegal' memory access. This might be an address outside the currently allowable segments or access modes not allowed for that segment.
- Transfer control to the operating system kernel using an interrupt or memory exception if an 'illegal' memory access occurs.

The memory mapping depends on memory management hardware in the computer, usually an integral part of the processor. It can follow two patterns, **segmented** or **paged**, or a combination of both.

CRUCIAL CONCEPT

Segmented memory management divides the address space into a few segments. They may be of different lengths and correspond to a particular usage of the memory space, say program or stack memory.

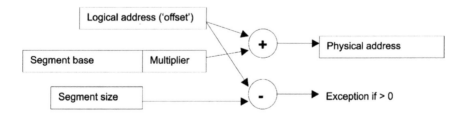

Segmented memory mapping

A **segment register** holds the base address of the segment and this is added to the data address (multiplied by some number to increase the addressing range of the computer), or **offset**, to give the **physical** address for the access. The physical address of segments must be on a boundary given by the multiplier. There may be a limit or size register for the segment.

The segment register may be selected using the top few bits of the logical address, or may be implicit in the encoding of the instruction as, for instance, in the case of the 'x86' architecture.

Paged memory management divides the address space into many **pages**. Pages are all of equal size (from 512 bytes to a few kilobytes). Allocation to different logical usage is done by management of the **page tables**.

A page table is simply a small (and fast) memory. The address of this memory is fed with the number of the page, the output of the memory provides the physical address of the page. The simplest way to derive the input to the page table is to choose the top part of the address, as shown below.

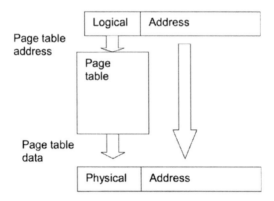

Additional data bits can be provided in the page table to give information about the page, for instance 'in use' or 'read only'. Violations cause a memory exception. A page table can be made to emulate most of the features of segmentation in the following way:

- the 'segment' is determined by the top bits of the logical address;
- the 'limit' of that segment is determined by marking the next page 'not in use'.

All memory allocations must be made in units of the page size. The page table can also 'relocate' individual pages, so that what appears to be a contiguous segment in logical memory may actually be spread all over physical memory, avoiding a large amount of copying from one area of memory to another to 'free up' a large continuous area.

Setting up a new segment means writing to a number of page table entries, whereas a segmentation scheme only requires the base and limit registers to be set up. A page table can be used as the second level to a segmented memory manager, as described above.

One of the functions of the hardware abstraction layer (see above) is to translate between the 'memory model' used by the operating system and that supported by the hardware. Sometimes it is not possible to hide the features of the hardware completely, leading to incompatibilities between versions of the same operating system running on different hardware.

Backing store means some slower, lower cost memory, typically magnetic disk, used to save the data in the main memory, which may be restored or swapped when needed.

Backing store programs which together use more than the system memory available may be run together, so long as there is sufficient backing store available to hold the data for all of the programs.

Virtual memory

Virtual memory depends on a small modification to the memory management schemes described above. If the processor is designed so that an instruction causing an exception may be executed again, or continued from the point where the exception was caused, then the kernel can swap the missing data from backing store into main memory and then re-run (or continue) the instruction, which will operate as though the missing data had been there all along.

Virtual memory can operate with either segmented or paged memory management schemes, but paged schemes have the advantage that as little as one page worth of the program's data need be in main memory at any time, whereas segmented schemes need the whole segment.

Section 4

File systems

The file system is the operating system component that allows us to keep track of the usage of the secondary storage of a computer (magnetic disks, CDs, DVDs and so on). Most file systems are structured around a few simple concepts, which are introduced here.

What file systems do

The secondary storage of a computer is so large that it is impracticable to access it using simple numerical addresses. It is desirable to provide some higher level abstraction for the structure of the computer's storage. This is called a file (by analogy with an office file).

CRUCIAL CONCEPT

A **file** is a named collection of data, stored on some secondary storage medium such as a magnetic disk. A file has a name, and may also have a number of **attributes** which control the use of the file.

Blocks and bytes

Although disks are organised as blocks of data, modern operating systems provide files that are an arbitrary length sequence of either characters or bytes. If an application requires a different structure (say, for instance a database program using data fields), then it is up to the programmer of that system to provide the required structure.

File systems

CRUCIAL CONCEPT

A **file system** is the name given to the means by which files are created, given names, read and written and deleted, and by which the real storage resources are allocated to files.

Typically an operating system will support a set of system calls to do with files, which will usually include the following operations:

- create a file; this operation will set up all of the file system structures necessary for the new file;
- name (or re-name) a file;
- read from a file;
- write to a file;

- delete a file; remove the filename, delete file system references to the file and return the storage blocks it used for re-use by new files.

Often there are several variants of each of these.

Section 5

Device management

An operating system allows your applications programs to work with whatever devices your computer has fitted, and allows you to change devices without rendering all your software obsolete.

CRUCIAL CONCEPT

A **device** is the name given to any piece of computer hardware outside the central CPU and main memory.

You can view the list of devices in a typical Windows PC by viewing the 'Device Manager', which you get at through the 'System' folder in the 'Control Panel'. An example is shown below.

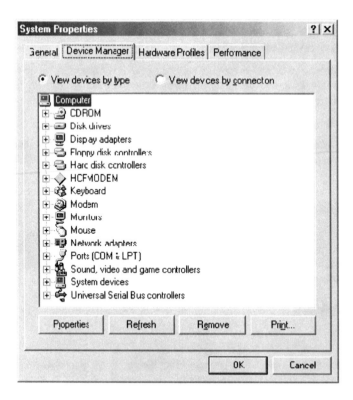

Why do they need managing?

Different types of device, as discussed in Chapter 6, can have very different requirements in terms of control and data timing. One of the things that an operating system must do is to provide the software that interfaces to a particular device, providing the applications programmer with a simpler model than the real device.

> ─── CRUCIAL CONCEPT ───
>
> **Device independence** is a feature of an API that frees applications programmers from having to program for a specific type or model of device. The API provides generic, standardised device interface definitions, such as block and stream devices and suitable graphics interface. This allows an applications program to run on a variety of hardware configurations without changing the hardware itself.

The operating system translates these standard commands into the sets of commands required by the real device hardware. The mechanism used by the operating system is called a device driver.

> ─── CRUCIAL CONCEPT ───
>
> A **device driver** is a software module within the operating system that translates from the generic device model provided in the API to the specific hardware requirements of a real device.

There are a number of ways of providing device drivers. They may be included in the kernel of the operating system or may be external to the kernel, the operating system being reconfigured by inclusion of the required drivers each time a device is fitted or changed.

Section 6

Process management and multi-tasking

Operating systems should be able to run several programs at once, without those programs interfering and stopping each other running.

> ─── CRUCIAL CONCEPTS ───
>
> A **process** or **task** is an individual program running on a computer. The program may be an applications program, or it may perform some function supporting the operating system. In a multi-tasking system the operating system is trying to create for each process the illusion that it has use of its own computer or **virtual machine**.

Maintaining a virtual machine depends on two things. The first is memory management, the second is sharing the single processor between processes. This is done by **time slicing,** whereby the processor runs a slice of the code for each process in turn, as follows. The **state** of a process, including the values of all variables and the next instruction to be executed, is stored on the process stack. To run a process the stack pointer of the processor is loaded with the address of the stack for that process and the top of the stack (the next instruction in that process) popped into the program counter. To stop a process (or **suspend** it) the address of the next instruction to be executed is pushed onto the stack and control passed to the **scheduler.**

> ─── CRUCIAL CONCEPT ───
>
> The **scheduler** is the operating system component in a multi-tasking o.s. which runs and suspends processes.

The scheduler keeps a number of lists, or queues, of processes, each identified by a pointer to the stack for that process. The queues are:

- running: this will contain one process only in a single processor machine;
- ready to run: these are processes that can run, but do not have use of the processor at the moment;
- waiting or suspended: these are processes that cannot run because they are waiting for something to happen, such as data to be received from a device.

The scheduler moves processes between these queues as they become ready to run or suspended and runs processes from the ready to run queue.

Processes are suspended when they cannot run any more, either the program has finished (in which case when it is suspended it will be deleted) or the process needs to wait for a device or another process (in which case it will be put on the suspended queue). Many operating systems operate **preemptive scheduling**, which means that after running for a certain short time a process will be suspended or preempted, whether or not is can still run. Preempted processes are placed back on the ready to run queue. Preemptive scheduling shares the available processor time between all processes, and results in a system with better interactive properties.

CRUCIAL CONCEPT

Processes need to communicate and co-operate, so the operating system must provide some means of **inter-process communication** which must provide both data communication and synchronisation. A common model used is to allow processes to pass messages to each other. In this model the inter-process communication may use the same system calls as communication via communication devices. The 'pipes' used in the Unix system is an example of this type of inter-process communication.

Another model is to provide a specific mechanism for propagation of 'events' between processes. Events encapsulate synchronisation and data and can be handled well in object oriented systems. Event based communication is typically used in modern WIMP systems.

Section 7

End of chapter assessment

Questions

1. The original 8086 processor had a segmentation scheme in which the value stored in a 16-bit segment register (called Code Segment or CS, Data Segment or DS, Stack Segment or SS and Extra Segment or ES) was multiplied by 16 and added to the 16-bit memory offset yielded by an instruction. Assuming the segment register values given in the table below (in hexadecimal), answer the following questions.

CS	0100h
DS	8721h
SS	FFF0h
ES	0000h

   a) What is the length of the memory address yielded by the segmentation operation, in bits?
   b) What is the physical address given by an offset of 0500h in the Code Segment?
   c) What is the physical address given by an offset of 0000h in the Data Segment?
   d) What offset in the Extra Segment gives the same physical address as 0100h in the Code Segement?
   e) What offset in the Extra Segment gives the same physical address as 0000h in the Stack Segment?

2. '32-bit' x86 processors have a paged memory management scheme with two levels of page table.

Virtual Address

31	21	11	0
Directory Offset	Page Table Offset	Page Offset	

The 32-bit virtual address is divided as follows:

a) The page offset uses bits 0-11, what is the size of a page?
b) The page table offset uses bits 12-21, how many pages in a page table?
c) What is the amount of memory represented by a page table?
d) The directory offset uses bits 22-31, how many page tables in the directory?

Answers

1. a) 16 bits multiplied by 16 (four bits) gives 20 bits
   b) $(0100h \times 10h) + 0500h = 01500h$
   c) $(8721h \times 10h) + 0000h = 87210h$
   d) Physical address in code segment $= (0100h \times 10h) + 0100h = 01100h$
      Base of Extra Segment $= (0000h \times 10h) = 00000h$
      Offset in Extra Segment $= 01100h - 00000h = 1100h$
   e) Physical address in stack segment $= (FFF0h \times 10h) + 0000h = FFF00h$
      Base of Extra Segment $= (0000h \times 10h) = 00000h$
      Offset in Extra Segment $= FFF00h - 00000h = FFF00h$; this is an invalid offset as it is larger than 16 bits

2. a) Field is 12 bits, number of bytes in a page $= 2^{12} = 4\ 096$
   b) Field is 10 bits, number of pages $= 2^{10} = 1\ 024$
   c) 1024 pages of 4096 bytes $= 2^{22} = 4\ 194\ 304$
   d) Field is 10 bits, number of page tables $= 2^{10} = 1\ 024$

Multiple-choice questions

1. What are the different layers of the onion skin model?
   a) hardware layers
   b) software layers
   c) fleshy layers
   d) abstraction layers
   e) program layers

2. Which of the following services is not provided by the Microsoft NT executive services layer?
   a) device drivers
   b) memory management
   c) executive massage
   d) window management
   e) graphics device interaction

3. What does API stand for?
   a) abstraction programming initialisation
   b) applications programming interface
   c) advanced protocol implementation
   d) applications protocol interface
   e) automatic plug-in

4. Which one of these would not normally be considered to be a 'device' in an operating system?
   a) laser printer
   b) magnetic disk drive
   c) CD-ROM drive

    d) system memory
    e) ethernet adapter

5. What is a 'device driver'?
    a) a specialist computer operator
    b) a type of control panel
    c) a diagnostic system for computer hardware
    d) a hardware installation system
    e) a software module interfacing to peripheral hardware

6. What is device independence a feature of (in an operating systems context)?
    a) the API
    b) magnetic disk drives
    c) a processor architecture
    d) a communications policy
    e) the CLI

7. What does CLI stand for?
    a) communications link interface
    b) command line interpreter
    c) customer liaison inspector
    d) computer link interface
    e) continuous line interval

8. Which is the missing word in the sentence 'WIMP user interfaces are based around a desktop _____ ?
    a) computer
    b) environment
    c) syntax
    d) metaphor
    e) simile

9. Which of the following is another term for a CLI?
    a) prompt
    b) MS-DOS
    c) legacy
    d) window
    e) shell

10. Which phrase describes the ability to run more than one program at the same time?
    a) multi-function
    b) interactive
    c) multi-tasking
    d) 32-bit
    e) new technology

11. What does a process stack store?
    a) the process state
    b) the clipboard
    c) program code
    d) discarded bytes
    e) free memory

12. Which one of these does *not* describe the possible state of a process?
    a) running
    b) illegal
    c) ready to run
    d) suspended
    e) waiting

Multiple-choice answers

1-d, 2-c, 3-b, 4-d, 5-e, 6-a, 7-b, 8-d, 9-e, 10-c, 11-a, 12-b.

Chapter 9
Program environments

Chapter summary

The aim here is to give you an overview of the API. Although some short program examples are included, they are intended to be illustrative, rather than learned themselves.

Learning outcomes

After studying this chapter you should aim to test your achievement by answering the multiple-choice questions and the examples at the end of the chapter. You should be able to do the following things.

Outcome 1: Be familiar with the type of operating systems resources available via an applications programming interface, and possess an overview of how these resources are accessed by programs.

Outcome 2: Understand the sequence of program operations necessary to access and use files and directories, and have an overview of the underlying data structures.

Outcome 3: Describe the 'file model' of I/O and be able to write program fragments which perform I/O to simple devices using it.

Outcome 4: Describe the concepts behind memory resource management, and locate where in program sources this function is likely to occur.

Outcome 5: Possess an overview of process instantiation, termination and inter-process communication in concurrent operating systems.

How will you be assessed on this?

Can you describe the sequence of creating, opening and using files? Can you write program fragments to do these things? Can you produce program fragments for common I/O operations? Can you recognise the symptoms of 'rogue' programs that don't release memory? Can you write simple program fragments to start and terminate programs and to communicate between them?

Useful information sources

Sun Java site including tutorials: http://java.sun.com/
Useful Windows API tutorials: http://www.relisoft.com/win32/, http://www.winprog.org/tutorial/

Section 1

The applications programming interface

We met the applications programming interface in Chapter 8. This recaps on that information, from a program's point of view.

What a program needs

The resources a program needs to run were discussed in Chapter 8. They are:

- program memory;
- stack memory (including data and heap memory);
- access to secondary storage (files);
- I/O.

These services are provided by the operating system and accessed by a program using the API. We have chosen to deal with one as an example, the Java API.
There will be several program fragments, in Java, to illustrate what is going on. You don't have to be familiar with Java programming, but you will need to know enough of it to recognise what is going on.

Section 2

File systems

This section should bring you to a level where you can read an API manual and understand the file operations being described.

We need to discuss file before I/O because the same API calls are used for both.

CRUCIAL CONCEPT

The **file model of I/O**: the Unix system introduced the idea of treating all input and output devices as files. All the work of translating this general input and output is handled by the device driver.

Filenames and directories

In the last chapter we left out any details of how we specify a particular file. We discuss this issue here.

CRUCIAL CONCEPT

A **file name** is a character string used to identify a file. It is unique in its own context, so that the file can be unambiguously identified.

Files are **persistent storage** – a file continues to exist after the program that created it stops running. When that happens, all the memory used by the program, which can be addressed directly by its address, is reallocated to another program. For the file to be accessed by many programs, we need a memory address independent way of identifying files, which is the file name.

> ────── CRUCIAL CONCEPT ──────
> The set of all possible names which may be given to files in a filing system is called its **name space**.

There are several factors affecting the name space of a file system. They are:

- the character set allowed to be used in file names;
- the number of characters allowed in a file name;
- any special purpose parts of a file name (for instance the file extension in the MS-DOS file system);
- any special treatment of particular file names (for instance, in the Unix file system, names beginning with '.' are 'invisible');
- the organisation of files into 'directories' or 'folders'.

Modern operating systems tend to allow very long file names which can include virtually all the characters on the keyboard.

> ────── CRUCIAL CONCEPT ──────
> A **directory** or **folder** is a means of grouping together a set of files.

Most operating systems treat a directory as a file which holds a list of filenames and references to those files.

- A file system may contain many directories.
- Directories may contain other directories; the file system becomes 'hierarchical', or tree-structured.

Filenames within a directory may be duplicated in other directories. To identify a file uniquely, you need to specify its name, the name of the directory it's in, the name of the directory that's in and so on, all the way back to the root. This is called the 'pathname'.

> ────── CRUCIAL CONCEPT ──────
> A **pathname** describes the 'path' to a file, running through every folder from the 'root' and ending in the name of the file itself. It forms a unique name within a computer system.

This pathname is written as a string of all the directory names, starting from the root, separated by some standard character. In Unix this character is '/', in the Microsoft systems it is '\'. A Unix pathname /users/bobn/workfiles/chap9 indicates a file called 'chap9', in the directory called 'workfiles' in the directory called 'bobn' in the directory called 'users' which is in the root directory.

Interfacing to a file

Each time a file is used within a program a data structure is necessary to store the current state of that file and to buffer data going to and from the file. Such a structure is called a 'file descriptor'.

> ────── CRUCIAL CONCEPT ──────
> A **file descriptor** is a data object in the memory space of a program. It contains all the information necessary to interface to a file that is in use.

Once a file descriptor has been created a reference to the descriptor serves as a reference to the file itself within the program. The file descriptor therefore serves as an interface between the program's memory address space and the file system name space.

Opening and closing files

CRUCIAL CONCEPT

If a file already exists, it needs to be 'opened', which changes its status to indicate that the file is in use. The file system needs to know which files are in use (for instance, to stop simultaneous writes to a file). Programs tell it this by **opening files** that they will use.

Using the Java API different classes are used to open files. We will look at the most general purpose, the RandomAccessFile.

```
RandomAccessFile file =
        new RandomAccessFile("/dir/filename", mode);
```

This opens the file indicated by the string /dir/filename, creates a file descriptor to hold its status and provides buffering from the file blocks to input and output objects. If there is no such file an exception is thrown. The mode parameter is 'r' if we just want to read, 'rw' if we want to write as well. An exception will be thrown if we can't perform the operation we want to (like, for instance, writing to a file that's already open for writing).

Reading and writing data

Once the file is open, reading is done using the read method.

```
int numread = file.read(buffer,offset,numtoread);
```

Buffer indicates the variable into which we want to read, **offset** indicates from where in the file we want to read (in bytes) and **numtoread** indicates how many bytes of data to read. The returned value is how many bytes have actually been read.

Similarly, data can be transferred into the file using the write method.

```
file.write(buffer,offset,numtoread);
```

If anything goes wrong an exception is raised.

Creating a new file

To create a file a directory entry for the file is created in a directory which maps the chosen file name to a data structure, held on a reserved part of the disk, containing the physical disk addresses for the disk blocks which form the file. This is called an 'inode' in Unix systems and a 'File Allocation Table' (FAT) in Microsoft systems. The inode also holds information about the file, the size, the owner and the access permissions. The same inode may be pointed at by several names in one or more directories, allowing a file to have several names or 'links'. At first the inode is empty, it will fill up as the file is written to. It can be linked to further lists of file blocks to enable the use of very large files.

In Java a file object is created which encodes the required name for the new file into a universal 'abstract filename' representation.

```
File myfile = new File("/new/dir/filename");
boolean status = myfile.CreateNewFile();
```

This operation creates a new file (directory entry and inode or FAT entry) with the filename given to myfile when it was instantiated. The return status is true if the file creation occurred properly.

Closing files

When a program has finished with a file it needs to 'close' it to return all the resources used as well as indicating to the operating system that the current operations have finished. In Java this is done simply by calling the close method of the open RandomAccessFile.

```
file.Close();
```

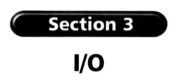

I/O

This section describes how I/O devices are handled in a modern API.

File I/O

The majority of programs can handle most of their device I/O in a device independent way, so long as they only want to handle generic functions, otherwise it means communicating directly with the device drivers.

The file model cannot overcome the limitations of the device itself. Thus it is impossible to read from a printer. Such attempts will result in either an exception being raised or else the request simply being ignored.

Devices are given standard file names. In Unix these devices files are held on a special directory (/dev), with a special inode that links to the relevant device driver. In Windows the special names are built in. To output a stream of characters to a printer using the Java API and the MS Windows operating system we first open the device file.

```
FileOutputStream printer = new FileOutputStream('LPT1');
```

FileOutputStream is designed particularly for stream output to files. LPT1 is Windows' special name for the primary printer connected to the system. If there is no printer, or the printer is unavailable for some other reason, a 'FileNotFound' exception will be raised.

Once the file (printer) has been opened, we can write data to it.

```
printer.write(buffer,numberofbytes)
```

Here **buffer** is the object containing the data we need to write, **numberofbytes** is the amount of data to be written.

Resource management

Here we look at the way memory resources are handled by an API.

Memory allocation

In Java 'heap memory' is allocated every time a new object is instantiated.

```
Someclass newobject = new Someclass();
```

This sequence creates a new instance of the class **Someclass**. An 'object' is actually a data structure. The 'new' call requests allocates enough memory for the data structure, if necessary requesting another chunk of memory from the operating system to make space for it. The data structure is initialised by the call of **SomeClass( )**.

When a data object is finished with, the memory that it uses must be released. Some APIs have a 'release' call. If a programmer forgets to call it, memory never gets released and ultimately the system runs out of memory. This 'memory leakage' is quite common with Windows programs.

CRUCIAL CONCEPT

The Java API uses **garbage collection**. Here the system keeps track of how many references (pointers) there are to an object. When the number falls to 0, indicating that it is no longer being used, the memory is released.

Section 5

Working with several programs

Modern operating systems are 'concurrent', they can run more than one program at the same time. This section introduces the API interface to concurrent process.

Starting and terminating programs

A program, such as a 'shell', must be able to start another program. The API provides a way of starting another named program. In Java, it's done like this.

```
Runtime r = Runtime.getRuntime();
Process newprocess = r.exec("command");
```

Here the method that starts the new process is **exec**, part of the **Runtime** class which we get by creating a new Runtime object, **r**. The parameter to **exec** is the name of the command (an 'executable' file) that the new process will execute.

CRUCIAL CONCEPT

An **executable file** is a file that contains program code, and can be loaded and run by the operating system. In Unix executable files are indicated by an 'x' file attribute. In Windows they are indicated by an 'exe', 'com' or 'bat' extension to the filename.

A new program environment is created, with memory allocated for its code, stack and variables. Into the code memory space is loaded the code in the named file, and the new program is started. The return value is a **Process** object, which can be used to gain information about and control over the new process. The Process object can be used to stop the new process running (also known as 'terminating' or 'killing' it).

```
newprocess.destroy();
```

When this method is called, the process represented by newprocess is terminated. Otherwise it will run until it comes to the end of the program or terminates itself, by calling the **exit** method of its own runtime. When a process dies, all memory and other resources that it uses are returned for re-use.

Concurrency

When a new process is started by default it is run concurrently with the process that started it. Concurrent processes can do more than one thing at once.

Sometimes what is needed is for the two programs to run sequentially. To do this, we 'suspend' the old process until the new process has finished, like this.

```
int result = newprocess.waitFor();
```

This causes the current process to halt until the new process has finished, a return value of 0 meaning successful completion.

Communicating between programs

There is a standard means of inputting and outputting data to and from other processes (and standard input and output devices, if necessary). In Java these are called the **standard input** (stdin), the **standard output** (stdout) and the **standard error** (stderr). They are effectively virtual input and output devices, and follow the convention of handling I/O as files.

A process that has created a new process can find its I/O streams using methods of the Process object.

```
OutputStream newstdin = newprocess.getOutputStream();
InputStream newstout = newprocess.getInputStream();
InputStream newstderr = newprocess.getErrorStream();
```

Note that the output stream (from the 'parent' process) is connected to the **stdin** of the new process. Once the parent has identified the stdin of the new process it can send it information.

```
newstdin.write(messageout);
```

'Messageout' holds the message to be sent. It is received in the new process by reading data from its stdin input stream, which is a property of a class called 'System'.

```
int bytesread = System.in.read(messagein);
```

The effect of the two operations will be to transfer the contents of the 'messageout' buffer in the parent process to the 'messagein' buffer in the child process. A message can be transferred in the other direction using **System.out.write** and **newstdout.read**.

Section 6

End of chapter assessment

Questions

1. If the CLI command to change the current working directory from the current directory to its parent (i.e. move up a level in the directory tree) is '**cd ..**', and the command to change the current directory to a directory **dir**, in the current directory, is '**cd dir**'; give a sequence of commands to change the current directory from /root/dira/dirb/branch1a/ branch1b/branch1c to /root/dira/branch2a/branch2b.

2. Give a Java program fragment that opens a file with pathname '/mydir/myfile', reads 100 bytes from the beginning of the file into a buffer named **buf** and closes the file again. Do not include any exception handling that may be necessary.

3. Give a Java program fragment that writes the contents of a 100 byte buffer called **buf** to a printer named 'LPT2'.

4. Give a Java program fragment that creates a new process executing the program 'ls .' and then waits for it to terminate.

5. Give a Java program fragment that creates a new process executing the program 'more', writes the contents of a 100 byte buffer called **buf** to the new process' standard input and then waits for the new process to terminate.

Answers

1. cd .. (to branch1b)
   cd .. (to branch1a)
   cd .. (to dirb)
   cd .. (to dira)
   cd branch2a
   cd branch2b

2.
```
RandomAccessFile myfile =
new RandomAccessFile("/mydir/myfile", "r");
int numread = myfile.read(buf,0, 100);
myfile.Close();
```

Note: This exercise is not about Java programming, don't worry if you have Java syntax errors as long as the sense is right (unless you're also doing a course in Java programming!).

3.
```
FileOutputStream printer = new FileOutputStream('LPT2');
printer.write(buf,100);
printer.Close();
```

4.
```
Runtime r = Runtime.getRuntime();
Process ls = r.exec("ls .");
int result = ls.waitFor();
```

5.
```
Runtime r = Runtime.getRuntime();
Process more = r.exec("more");
OutputStream morestdin = newprocess.getOutputStream();
morestdin.write(buf,100);
int result = more.waitFor();
```

Multiple-choice questions

1. Which one of these does a program not require in order to run?
   a) machine code
   b) compiler
   c) input devices or files
   d) output devices or files
   e) stack memory

2. Which one of these is the Java API supported by?
   a) machine code
   b) compiler
   c) JVM
   d) J++
   e) Java beans

3. Which of the terms may be used to describe the type of storage provided by files?
   a) persuasive
   b) perquisite
   c) perceivable
   d) persistent
   e) percentile

4. What would you expect to happen if a call of `RandomAccessFile("q4file", "rw")` is made, and the file `g4file` has a 'read only' attribute?
   a) the file is opened for reading only
   b) the file is opened for reading and writing
   c) the file is opened for writing only
   d) an exception is thrown
   e) the application is terminated

5. What is the value returned by the 'write' method of the 'file' class?
   a) none
   b) number of bytes written
   c) number of characters written
   d) the status of the file
   e) the size of the file

6. What is the name of the data structure containing disk block addresses in the Unix system?
   a) FAT
   b) NTFS
   c) inode
   d) dnode
   e) fnode

7. What is a method used to initialise a new instance of a class (in Java) called?
   a) instantiator
   b) initialiser
   c) opener
   d) starter
   e) constructor

8. What mechanism does the Java API use to prevent 'memory leakage'?
   a) garbage collection
   b) error detection
   c) error detection and correction
   d) silicone
   e) parity

9. What is the name of the method of 'Runtime' used to start a new process?
   a) start
   b) newProcess
   c) startProcess
   d) exec
   e) execute

10. What is the term used to describe the input stream of a Unix process?
   a) input
   b) normal input
   c) standard input
   d) stream input
   e) data input

Multiple-choice answers

1-b, 2-b, 3-d, 4-d, 5-a, 6-c, 7-e, 8-a, 9-d, 10-c.

Chapter 10
The user interface

Chapter summary

This chapter extends our study of APIs by looking specifically at the part to do with the user interface.

Learning outcomes

After studying this chapter you should be able to do the following things.

Outcome 1: **Know the term 'user interface' and be able to describe the system functions which comprise it and understand the importance of consistency, predictability and use of metaphor and feedback.**

Outcome 2: **Have an overview of and know the basics of use of a command line interpreter style of user interface, use of prompts, commands and dialogue design.**

Outcome 3: **Demonstrate a basic understanding of the design issues and use of windowed user interfaces, and be able to describe the API features on which simple window operations depend.**

How will you be assessed on this?

Practical work can include using user interfaces and programming using the user interface part of a particular API. The use of a CLI may be tested by using a 'skills test' or by answering questions. For windowed UIs you should be able to describe the function of simple programs and the steps necessary to produce simple UI functions using an API such as Java Swing.

Useful information sources

Horton, W. *The Icon Book*, John Wiley, ISBN 0-471-59900-X.
Fowler, S. (1998) *GUI Design Handbook*, McGraw-Hill, New York. ISBN 0-07-059274-8.
Sun Java site including tutorials: http://java.sun.com/

Section 1

User interface systems

Here we look at the two main styles of user interface design in operating systems.

User interface design

Modern operating systems place great emphasis on usability, and a major part of the code (and computer resources) are directed at supporting the 'user interface'.

—— CRUCIAL CONCEPT ——

The **user interface** of an operating system is the means by which the user gives instructions to the operating system and receives information from it.

The oldest and simplest way of receiving commands from the user is called a command line interpreter, or shell.

—— CRUCIAL CONCEPT ——

A **command line interpreter** (CLI) or 'shell' is a program that accepts operating system commands from the user in the form of text, interprets those commands and passes those commands on to the operating system.

Commands issued to a command line interpreter must have some formal structure or syntax, like a programming language, and if this syntax is designed in a regular and simple way it makes the CLI much easier to use. If correctly constructed the command is passed to the operating system proper for action, otherwise there is an error message.

—— CRUCIAL TIP ——

Feedback to the user is essential for a satisfactory user interface. In a CLI the feedback is primarily in the form of error or information messages.

Well designed CLIs can provide very good user interface characteristics, particularly for knowledgeable users.

—— CRUCIAL CONCEPT ——

WIMP stands for windows, icons, menus, pointer. It receives commands by movement of a mouse guide pointer and selection of icons and menus. Multiple **windows** allow several programs to share the screen at once.

Shown below is my computer screen as I type this. It's a typical example of a WIMP system.

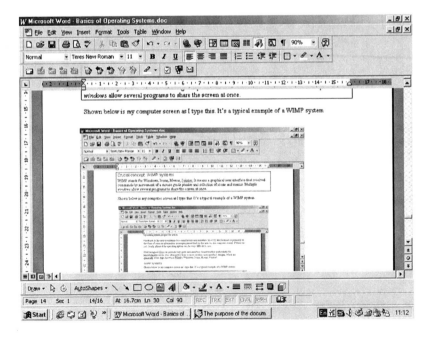

This is essentially doing the same job as a command line interpreter but the commands are composed of actions on icons and menus produced by moving and clicking the (mouse)

pointer. If I enter a properly formed command, the command is passed on to the operating system, which either takes appropriate action itself, or passes the command to the application program.

Command dialogue design

CRUCIAL CONCEPT

The **command dialogue** is the interchange of information that occurs between user and computer via the user interface. It may be a textual dialogue, using a CLI, or a graphical one, using a WIMP system.

The usability of both CLIs and WIMPs depends on how carefully the command dialogue has been designed. The user needs a clear 'mental model' of how the system will respond to instructions. To help with this the command dialogue needs three characteristics.

1. It must be consistent – the same type of operation occurs in the same way, the rules of construction of similar commands are the same.
2. It must be predictable – the user needs to have some idea of what the likely outcome of any action is.
3. It must provide feedback as to what it's doing, so the user gains confidence about the effect of commands.

A 'metaphor' can help underline the user's mental model that the UI designer intended. An example of this is the use of 'tabs' to select multiple pages of a dialogue. They look and behave like tabs in a card file, so the user understands how to interact with it. Metaphor can be used in textual user interfaces as well.

Section 2

Command line user interfaces

CLIs have not become completely redundant in modern computer systems. This section is an overview of the design and implementation of command line based user interfaces.

Basics of CLIs

CRUCIAL CONCEPT

A **prompt** is a string of characters placed at the screen at the beginning of the command line to prompt the user to enter their part of the command dialogue, the command to be executed. It can also provide feedback about the current state of the system, and therefore what a command will do.

In most operating systems, the prompt given by the CLI can be changed by the user to be either a constant string or some system information, such as the current working directory. The prompt string conventionally finishes with a character which is intended to suggest to the user 'your turn to type', often > or :. A typical prompt, giving the current shell program, might be:

```
bash:
```

This is one of the CLIs available for Unix. After the prompt, the user is expected to type the command to be executed.

```
bash: ls↵
```

The 'newline' (⏎) is shown explicitly, although it would be invisible on the screen. The bash program searches in some directories (it knows where to look from an 'environment variable' called PATH) for an 'executable' file called 'ls', which it loads and runs, waiting until 'ls' has terminated before continuing. Bash sends the output of 'ls' (a directory listing program) to the screen and then sends a new prompt ready for the next command.

```
bash: ls⏎
thisfile  thatfile  anotherfile
bash:
```

Suppose the user had wanted to list a named directory rather than the current one. To do this, the directory is named as an argument string.

CRUCIAL CONCEPT

An **argument string** is a string of characters to the right of the program name in a CLI command. It provides parameter information to the program to configure it when it runs.

```
bash: ls mydir⏎
mydirfile1 mydirfile2
bash:
```

The argument string is passed to a program and placed in its program environment by the shell. It is up to the programmer of the ls program what is done with that argument string.

Another option on the command line are 'switches'. For instance, 'ls' can be configured to display full details about each file, as follows.

```
bash: ls -l mydir⏎
-rw-rw-r-  1 bob
staff 1035 March 17 20:25 mydirfile1
-rw-rw-r-  1 bob
staff 221 March 17 20:31 mydirfile2
bash:
```

Here the 'switch' is '-l' (for long listing).

A single CLI command can send a large amount of information to the program on one command line. To use them efficiently the user has to remember all the parameters and switches for each particular program. They can't readily handle interaction while the program is running.

The solution to this is to provide the program itself with a CLI. It is useful if the user knows that interaction is with the program, not the shell. This could be done with a 'banner' or a distinctive prompt, such as the program's name.

```
bash: cldemo⏎
- - -  cldemo program v27.03a  - - -
cldemo: hello⏎
Hi there.
cldemo: goodbye⏎
- - -  cldemo program v27.03a terminating  - - -
bash:
```

The user has to remember all the commands for this program as well, so it's useful to make them clear and consistent in style with the CLI for the underlying operating system.

Section 3

Windowed user interfaces

Most modern computers use a windowed user interface. This section introduces you to the API functions on which they depend and the operating systems functions supporting the API.

Overview of a windowed user interface

Fundamentally a windowed user interface is no more 'intuitive' than a textual one, but it does give more opportunity for use of metaphor as an aid to memorising all the commands. Generally this metaphor is based around a few ideas.

- A desktop. The screen displays a 'desktop' on which pieces of paper are placed. They overlay each other and can be moved around the desktop and can be resized.
- Windows. Each 'piece of paper' is actually a 'window' onto something else. The window might let the user see the whole of the something else, or a small portion.
- Menu. When there are a lot of commands they can be selected from a menu, which displays all the available options.
- Folders. Instead of 'directories' we have 'folders' which contain sets of documents and other objects, including other folders.
- Various command metaphors such as 'sliders', 'pushbuttons', and 'radio buttons'.

Windowed systems are inherently more concurrent than CLI systems, because the user can see several windows open at once.

Programming a windowed user interface is more complex than a CLI. For this reason windowed user interfaces have a complex support library behind them. For the discussion that follows we'll use the MS Windows system as an example of what the windows look like and do, and the Java Swing API for any program examples we need.

Basic operations

Let's start off by looking at the equivalent of the 'ls' command in MS Windows. The user opens a folder by clicking on folder 'icon' within another folder.

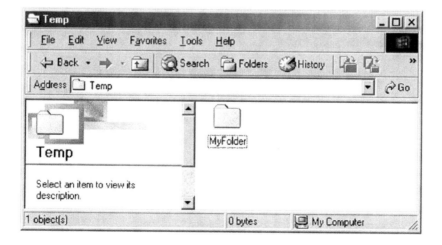

CRUCIAL CONCEPT

An **icon** is a compact graphical representation of an object. An icon can be 'opened', usually by double clicking on it, to display a window holding the complete object.

Each icon displayed on the screen has an associated data structure which tells the system what kind of object this represents. We can see some of the information contained in this data structure by looking at the icon's 'properties'.

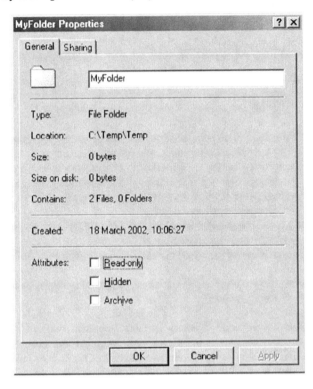

From the window displayed we can see that MyFolder is a file folder and contains two files. If we double click on the MyFolder icon, the system looks up the properties of the icon to see what it represents. It selects a suitable application program to run to 'open' the icon. A command line is made up consisting of the name of the program to run (Explorer), along with the folder to open (MyFolder) as a parameter (you can do this manually, start up a 'MS-DOS Prompt'– the Windows CLI – and type 'explorer foldername'). 'Explorer' is the Windows equivalent of the 'ls' program. When it runs it displays a new window containing an icon for each file in the folder.

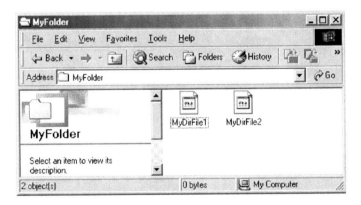

The various controls and menus around the window allow us to configure the explorer to our needs.

The Explorer also acts as a 'shell', in that it can start new programs. Double clicking on an icon starts a program running, according to the following rules:

- if the file is executable (has a .exe or .bat extension) it is run;
- if the file is not executable, but has a program associated with its file extension, then that program is run, with the file name as a parameter;
- if there is no associated program then an 'open with' dialogue is started up, which asks the user to select a program from a list.

Section 4

API of windowed user interfaces

This section is intended to give a flavour of a window API.

A working example

For this section we will look at how a very simple directory listing program, like Explorer, operates. The Swing API is typical of windowed APIs that are designed in an 'object oriented' style.

Creating a new window

We define our new program as a subclass of the type of window that we want to display, as follows:

```
1.  public class FolderDemo extends JPanel {
2.
3.  static JFrame frame;
4.
5.    static public void main(String args[]) {
6.
7.       FolderDemo panel = new FolderDemo(args[0]);
8.
9.       frame = new JFrame("FolderDemo");
10.      frame.addWindowListener(new WindowAdapter() {
11.       public void windowClosing(WindowEvent e) {System.exit(0);}
12.       });
13.      frame.getContentPane().add(panel);
14.      frame.pack();
15.      frame.setVisible(true);
16.   }
17. }
```

Line 1 defines our program to be a new class called FolderDemo that extends the class Jpanel, which includes the methods for displaying and organising a window. This ensures that the class too includes all the required methods. The new class implements ActionListener. This is a Java protocol that defines how interaction actions such as keypresses and mouse clicks are handled.

Line 3 defines a class JFrame, which will provide the surround or frame our window. Starting in line 5 is the main() method that is called by the operating system when our program is run. The parameter args is an array of argument values. The first will give the name of the directory to be displayed.

Line 7 creates the object that holds the state of this panel, called 'panel', giving it the name of the directory being listed.

Line 9 creates the object to hold the state of the window frame, called 'frame'. The JFrame constructor is given the name of the folder to be displayed as a parameter, which will result in this window having that folder name displayed in its top banner.

Lines 10 and 11 add in an 'action listener' of a type, 'window listener'. When the user makes some interaction, the operating system will find out from the location on the screen which object that relates to and send an 'action message'. This is a method that will react to that action message, a 'windowClosing' action. The method calls System,exit(0) to close the window and release all its resources.

Line 13 fits the panel we defined in line 2 into the frame we have just defined and line 14 causes the frame to automatically size itself to fit snugly round the panel. The data that will make up the image of the frame and its contents has now all been set up, but it only exists in the program's memory. Line 15 makes it visible, which means that the window system assembles the image into the display memory, taking into account any other windows that might overlap or obscure it. Whenever the new window needs to be redrawn, the data to recreate it exists in the objects we have just created.

The 'listeners' remain active, responding to user actions until the program is terminated by the windowClosing action. This is a style of programming known as 'event driven programming'.

Displaying information

We haven't seen how information is displayed in the window. This is done within the FolderDemo constructor, which is shown here.

```
1.  public FolderDemo (String arg) {
2.      File folder = new File(arg);
3.      if (folder.isDirectory()) {
4.          String[] files = folder.list();
5.          final JList list = new JList(files);
6.          MouseListener mouseListener = new MouseAdapter() {};
7.          list.addMouseListener(mouseListener);
8.          add(list);
9.      } else {
10.         JLabel msg = new JLabel(arg.concat(" is not a folder."));
11.         add (msg);
12.     }
13. }
```

Line 1 declares this constructor, the argument string is passed from the main program. Line 2 declares a File object, which is set to the filename passed in arg. In line 3 the file is checked to see if it's a directory. If so, we use the method 'list' built into the File object to produce a list of files that it contains.

Line 5 declares a window object list, which is of class JList, designed for displaying lists of values, here file names. Line 6 attaches a 'mouse listener' to this object (the ellipsis stands for the definition of the mouseListener, which is discussed in the next section). This will be called if the mouse clicks over the image of the object 'list' on the screen. In line 8 we add this new list object into the panel we are building. This is what the new window looks like.

Line 10 is executed if the file is not a directory. It constructs a JLabel object saying that the file is not a directory and attaches this to the panel in line 11. In this case, when the window is displayed all it will contain is this window.

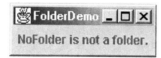

Events and controls

Here is the 'mouse listener' that we attached to the list of filenames.

```
1.  MouseListener mouseListener = new MouseAdapter() {
2.    public void mouseClicked(MouseEvent e) {
3.      String command;
4.      String filename;
5.      File file;
6.      Process child;
7.      Runtime r = Runtime.getRuntime();
8.      if (e.getClickCount() == 2) {
9.        list.setSelectedIndex(list.locationToIndex(e.getPoint()));
10.     filename = (String) list.getSelectedValue();
11.     file = new File(filename);
12.     if (file.isDirectory()) {
13.       command = new String("java FolderDemo ");
14.     } else {
15.       command = new String("Viewer ");
16.     }
17.     try {
18.       child = r.exec(command.concat(filename));
19.     } catch (IOException ioe) {
20.     }
21.     }
22.   }
23. };
```

Line 1 declares it as a being created from the MouseAdapter class. In Line 2 we define the method for this class 'mouseClicked', it will be called when the mouse is clicked. Line 8 checks the event e, passed as a message when the action occurs, to see that the click count is 2, only count double clicks. Line 9 finds the list item over which the mouse was clicked and selects it, using the setSelecteIndex method of list. Line 10 retrieves the filename in the selected list entry. Lines 11 and 12 check whether this file is a directory. If so the string command is set to be FolderDemo, otherwise it is set to be 'viewer'. Lines 13–20 start a new program, with the filename as a parameter. If the file was a directory, what we get is another copy of the FolderDemo program. Otherwise it's an application called 'Viewer'.

Section 5

End of chapter assessment

Multiple-choice questions

1. What does 'CLI' stand for?
   a) clean line interface
   b) completely lunatic interface
   c) command line interpreter
   d) cleverly loaded integer
   e) context level initialisation

2. What is used to provide a user with information about what a user interface is doing?
   a) outback
   b) feedback
   c) front-to-back
   d) hatchback
   e) lunchpack

3. What does 'WIMP' stand for?
   a) windows irritates more people
   b) windowed interface multiple panes
   c) windows interfaced mouse pointer
   d) windows, icons, menus, pointer
   e) worry interval measured in picoseconds

4. Which one of these is used to reinforce a user's 'mental model' of the operation of a user interface?
   a) metaphor
   b) simile
   c) smile
   d) alliteration
   e) illiteration

5. Which part of a CLI command dialogue tells the user to enter a command?
   a) beep
   b) click
   c) caret
   d) carrot
   e) prompt

6. Which part of a CLI command dialogue allows parameter information to be passed to a program?
   a) prompt
   b) argument string
   c) feedback
   d) floppy disk
   e) keyboard

7. What is an icon?
   a) an acronym for 'interface centred operating network'
   b) a pointer that moves with the mouse
   c) a brand of camera
   d) a compact graphical representation of an object
   e) a representation of a button

8. What is Java Swing?
   a) the Java music API
   b) a Java window system API
   c) the Java corporate song
   d) the Java network API
   e) the Java notebook API

9. What is the name of the Java Swing object that provides the surround to a window?
   a) JSurround
   b) JEdge
   c) JBorder
   d) JFrame
   e) JOutside

10. What is the Java Swing interface that captures user interaction?
   a) user interface
   b) action interface
   c) action listener
   d) user listener
   e) interface listener

Multiple-choice answers

1-c, 2-b, 3-c, 4-a, 5-e, 6-b, 7-d, 8-b, 9-d, 10-c

Chapter 11
Local networks and distributed systems

Chapter summary

Almost all computers today are 'networked', or part of a 'distributed system'. This section takes an overview of networking, and gives a basic description of network technology.

Learning outcomes

After studying this chapter you should aim to test your achievement by answering the multiple-choice questions and the examples at the end of the chapter. You should be able to do the following things.

Outcome 1: Explain what is needed for an electrical circuit.
Outcome 2: Explain the advantages and disadvantages of different types of electrical data cable.
Outcome 3: Explain principles of operation of optical fibres.
Outcome 4: Explain the advantages and disadvantages of optical fibre.
Outcome 5: Explain the benefits of LANs.
Outcome 6: Distinguish between peer-to-peer and client-server networks.
Outcome 7: Explain what is meant by the Internet.

How will you be assessed on this?

Assessment of this is probably on the basis of facts, which may well be assessed using multiple-choice questions.

Useful information sources

The Development of Communication Networks http://www.rad.com/networks/1994/networks/preface.htm
The OSI Seven Layer Model http://www.rad.com/networks/1997/nettut/protocols.html#OSI7
The Internet Engineering Taskforce http://www.ietf.org
Introduction to the Internet Protocols http://oac3.hsc.uth.tmc.edu/staff/snewton/tcp-tutorial

Section 1

Circuits, signals and communication

This section describes the process of communication using electrical signals and the important terms used to describe the quality of communication media.

> CRUCIAL CONCEPT
>
> If a battery has a wire going from one of its ends to one terminal of a light bulb the bulb will not light. But if a second wire is connected from the other end of the battery to the other terminal of the light bulb the bulb will light. This shows that a complete **electric circuit** is needed.

The battery provides the electro-motive force (e.m.f.) needed to cause a current to flow around the circuit and the current flowing through the bulb causes it to shine. The e.m.f. is usually provided by a mechanical generator, usually in a power station. These generators make use of the fact that moving charges (current) create a magnetic field and that a varying magnetic field creates a current, a principle that will be important in our discussion of noise problems in communication.

Signals, noise and cables

> CRUCIAL CONCEPTS
>
> If in our simple circuit with battery and bulb we have a switch at a distance from the bulb, we can switch the bulb on and off to signal to someone near the bulb. We have 'encoded' a **signal** onto the current in the wire.
>
> As the length of the electric circuit gets longer so the strength of the signal gets weaker. This is called **attenuation**. Attenuation (and amplification) is measured in decibels. A reduction in signal strength to one half its previous value is about –3 decibels. So 3 decibels is an increase of two times and 6 decibels, an increase of four times.
>
> **Noise** is a term for unwanted signals that appear on a communication link.

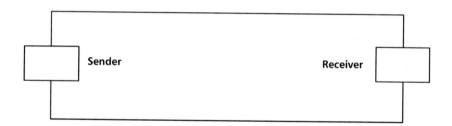

If a sender and receiver of electrical signals are arranged in a circuit as above it is quite likely that there will be changing magnetic fields through the circuit, possibly caused by other communications cable or electrical and electronic equipment, which will tend to cause electric currents to flow in the circuit. This 'induced' current is **noise**.

If the circuit were to be twisted as shown below, any increase in the downward magnetic field over the whole of the circuit would tend to produce a clockwise current in both halves of the circuit and this would cancel out over the whole circuit. A reduction in the size of the loops will also reduce the effect.

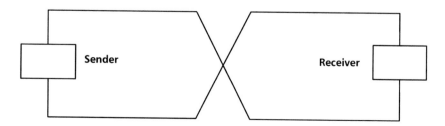

The most common cable installed today uses this principle. **Unshielded twisted pair** (UTP) has four pairs of wires. The specification normally used is **Category 5e** which defines the thickness of the wires, the thickness and material of the insulation, and the amount of twist in the different twisted pairs. (The four pairs are twisted by different amounts so that signals from one pair are not picked up by another pair.)

Another way of reducing noise pickup is to make one of the conductors completely surround the other. This cable is called co-axial cable. This has two beneficial effects - the outer conductor shields the space within as magnetic fields have difficulty penetrating a conductor, and also any magnetic field which does penetrate will pass both sides of the internal conductor so that the effects will tend to cancel out. It is more expensive and more difficult to install than UTP. A system which gives some of the advantages of both is **shielded twisted pair** (STP) which is specified for IBM token ring networks. It has a layer of aluminium foil wrapped around the twisted pairs. The main disadvantage of STP is the increased cost of the cable.

Reflection

Whenever a signal, electric, optic or radio, moves from one material to another (a change of thickness of wire, spacing of conductors, change of insulation, change of type of glass in fibre optics) there will be a reflection of the signal. The amount of reflection depends on the amount of the change and great care is taken in the design of connectors to minimise this effect. The characteristic quantity which describes this change in electric circuits is the **impedance**, and in optical systems the **refractive index**. It is important to take great care when assembling connectors that you do not introduce additional reflections because of the poor quality of the joint. The reflection also reduces the amount of signal going forward i.e. adding to the attenuation. Reflections were a serious problem on co-axial cable as the reflections arrived after the signal and behaved like noise and could mean that the **network interface card** (NIC) could not reliably decode the signal.

CRUCIAL CONCEPT

If two circuits are close to each other the signal in one circuit will produce a changing magnetic field which may be picked up by the other circuit. This is called **cross-talk**. If this happens so that a transmitting device sees its own signal from one pair coming back on another pair this is called near end cross talk or NEXT.

If two circuits are required between the same end points it is possible for them to share the same return path. In fact it is also possible for a circuit, or circuits, to use the 'earth' or 'ground' as the return path.

Two independent electricity supplies may have quite different voltages which could damage interconnected equipment or even be dangerous to humans. When connecting between devices which could be on different power supplies we should use fibre optics as these are not a conductor of electricity. This is likely to be in different buildings or sometimes on different floors of the same building.

Fibre optics

When light travels in a vacuum it travels at about 300,000 km per second. It travels slightly slower than this in air and about two thirds as fast as this in glass or in water. The ratio of the speed in a vacuum and the speed in a material is called the refractive index (RI) of the material. When light goes at an angle from a material with one RI to another with a different RI it changes direction. If the light is in a material with a high RI and it meets the boundary with a material of lower RI at a sufficiently shallow angle it does not go into the low RI material but totally reflects at the boundary. If light is sent into the end of a glass rod it will bounce off the sides and appear at the other end of the rod with no light coming out of the sides, if the surface of the rod is perfect and has no scratches. The surface of the rod may be protected by encasing it in a different glass with a lower refractive index. If we heat this composite rod until the glass goes soft, and draw it out until it is about as thick as a human hair, we have an optical fibre. Optical fibres can be made from plastic but they are not as good as glass. With glass the –3db point (half input brightness) is tens of kilometers. They are used in one direction only and it is usually the case that several strands are installed within the same outer cover.

Multi-mode optical fibre

The fibre core is either 62.5 μm or 50 μm diameter. (The latter is one 20th of a millimeter.) At this diameter light which travels down the centre of the fibre reaches the other end before light which zigzags along the fibre. This is called dispersion and limits the distance or data rate that can be used. The more commonly used 62.5 μm can theoretically carry 700 Mbps (700 megabits per second) over a distance of one kilometre while the 50 μm can carry 1 Gbps (1 gigabit per second = 1000 Mbps) over the same distance. The standards specify rather shorter distances than these at 1 Gbps.

Single-mode fibre

This fibre has a core diameter of 8 μm and consequently there is only one way that light can travel along the cable (this may seem strange but it is a quantum effect and they are often strange). It is currently not known what the maximum data rate is for single-mode fibre – it is truly huge. Single-mode fibre is used for long haul routes such as the undersea cables from Europe to America and from America across the Pacific to Japan as well as between telephone exchanges. The signal is amplified by optical amplifiers, within special glass sections.

Radio communication

This uses electro-magnetic waves to carry signals. Radio uses a variety of techniques to encode the information onto the radio waves. The earliest method was to simply switch the waves on and off using Morse Code. Long and medium wave radio uses AM = amplitude modulation. FM radio uses VHF/FM = very high frequency/frequency modulation. The most recent method for Broadcast radio is to encode the sound using digital techniques including QAM (Quadrature Amplitude Modulation).

Electro-magnetic waves are given different names depending on their wavelength or frequency – from gamma rays through X-rays, ultra-violet, light, infra-red waves, microwaves, UHF = ultra high frequency radio, VHF, medium wave, long wave, ultra low frequency. Cell phones use UHF digital signals. Satellite communication uses microwave digital signals to communicate from a ground station via the satellite which receives the signal and retransmits it to the destination ground station. Low power radio can also be used to create wireless LANs.

Section 2

What is a LAN?

This section describes local area networks (LANs).

───── CRUCIAL CONCEPT ─────

A **local area network** (LAN) is a collection of devices in a small geographic area that are connected together so that they can communicate with each other. Usually there will be personal computers (PCs) but there may also be servers and/or printers and/or scanners.

What are LANs used for?

In business many people need to access the same information. Sales people need to have access to customer information and so do the people preparing accounts. LANs provide that connectivity. Many computer users require access to printing facilities but not all the time and a LAN makes it possible to share this type of resource. Access to the Internet is becoming much more common in the home, many households have more than one computer and a small network allows shared access to this resource.

LAN technologies

Ethernet

The most common technology is the Ethernet LAN. In its original form it consisted of a length of thick co-axial cable, up to 500 m in length with devices (usually PCs) connected into this cable. This topology is referred to as a bus. If a greater length than this was required up to four repeaters could be added making the total length of the LAN 2.5 km in length. The repeaters simply transmitted a signal arriving on one side of the repeater to the other side. Every device on the network could receive every message sent. The data rate was fairly quickly standardised at 10 Mbps. This technology is described as 10Base5 i.e. 10 Mbps, Baseband (not a modulated signal) 5 x 100 m segment length. Each device attached to the network must have a network interface Card (NIC) installed in order to communicate on the network.

A cheaper alternative was introduced which also used co-axial cable but thinner and cheaper, and this had a maximum length between repeaters of 200 m. Otherwise it was very similar – 10Base2 i.e. 10 Mbps Baseband 2 x 100 m segment length.

The current technology is to use UTP cable which is not connected as a bus but is connected using a multi-port repeater which is called a **hub**. The cable length is reduced to about 100 m. This topology looks like a star, but behaves like a bus as all devices attached to the hub receive all messages sent to the hub. Many devices these days have NICs which can communicate at either 10 Mbps or 100 Mbps and can detect automatically if they are on a network which supports the higher speed. Referred to as 10BaseT or 100 BaseT i.e. 10 (or 100) Mbps Baseband Twisted pair.

Token Ring

IBM introduced a different LAN arrangement where the machines are arranged in a ring. As with Ethernet every computer receives every message but only takes note of those addressed to it. The data rate is either 4 Mbps or 16 Mbps, the former can use UTP but the latter requires shielded twisted pair (STP). Each computer is attached, by a repeater, to the ring. There may be up to 250 repeaters.

Token Bus

This LAN technology was developed for General Motors for a manufacturing environment. It uses a co-axial cable bus with each of the computers attached to this bus.

--- CRUCIAL CONCEPT ---

Media access control: when there are more than two devices connected to a shared medium there must be some control of access to the medium.

With Token Ring a special, very small data packet, called a token, is passed round the ring and when a device has a message to send it waits for this token and changes it into a start of frame delimiter, by changing one bit. It then adds some additional information including destination address, source address, the data and the frame check sequence. This is sent round the ring. Each computer looks to see if its address is the destination and the destination computer then copies the data and changes one or two bits at the end of the frame. When the source machine has finished and has received the frame header, having circulated the ring, it transmits a new token. In normal operation there are no collisions and under heavy load every machine gets its fair share.

With Token Bus the network behaves in a similar way but the token is passed around a logical ring. Organising a logical ring on a physical bus requires quite complex software to decide at the outset which machine is at the start of the logical ring and how the devices are arranged in sequence. If a device is going to leave the ring it must tell its upstream neighbour the address of its downstream neighbour so that the ring is maintained. If a machine is switched off without doing this the system must be able to cope with the problem. As with Token Ring the system is fair and reliable under heavy load.

The media access control for an Ethernet network is called CSMA/CD, which stands for 'carrier sense multiple access with collision detection'. The devices on the network listen to the network (carrier sense) and will not interrupt if a signal is detected. However, it is possible for two devices to start transmission at a sufficiently small interval that the signal from one has not reached the other when it starts transmitting. When two signals are on the network together neither will be successfully received and we say a collision has occurred. On a co-axial cable network a device which is transmitting can detect that another transmission is present (collision detection) and it will then continue transmission with a 'jam' signal for a short time and then cease transmission and wait for silence and a random period of time before trying again. To ensure that collisions are always detected by both transmitting devices, there is a minimum frame size. Using UTP and hubs at 10 Mbps one twisted pair is used to transmit and another pair to receive and the other two pairs are unused. All four pairs are used in various ways at the higher speeds and some NICs support **full duplex** communications, which is transmission in both directions simultaneously. If an Ethernet device needs to transmit a frame it may always find another transmission on the network. There is no guarantee that it will ever transmit. This is why it is considered to be unusable in a manufacturing environment. Also if the network is overloaded it may fail, slowing down to an unusable crawl, because each collision means that two frames have to be transmitted later. Users exacerbate this by re-sending messages which have not gone through quickly enough.

Section 3

Types of information systems using LANs

This section deals with two different ways of organising services on a LAN.

CRUCIAL CONCEPT

The simplest of networked systems are **peer-to-peer LANs**, that is each PC is equal in importance, there are no special 'servers', although not all of the machine necessarily provide the same services.

One of them may have a modem installed allowing connection to a telephone line and hence to an ISP (Internet Service Provider) and the Internet. Another may have a printer attached that the other may access. They may make some of their file systems accessible to other PCs in the little network. The PCs collaborate to share each other's resources. The advantage of this system is the low cost and simplicity. The disadvantage is that a PC may slow down significantly while another user is using its facilities, and if the user of a PC causes it to stop working (a program crash or just switches it off) the other users are unable to use its services. Past a certain size peer-to-peer networks become difficult to manage, because the services are spread all over the place.

CRUCIAL CONCEPT

A better arrangement for larger systems is to have dedicated computers (called servers) provide one or more of the important services and the users access whichever service they require as clients. These are client-server LANs.

Typical servers are file servers (which provide data storage for the machines on the network), print servers (which provide centralised printing services) and gateways to exterior, wide area networks such as the Internet. Depending on the demands likely to be made of them a server may provide just one service or several services. Because the server is not being used as a user's machine, there is much less risk of it failing in its task, and the system administrator can pay particular attention to file backup, servicing and so on. Also, its specification may be more accurately attuned to its task.

Section 4

Connecting up your LAN

This section deals with methods and techniques for building a small LAN. There is quite a lot of practical detail here, to provide you with enough background information to be able to do the job.

Building a LAN

Most new LANs are connected up using UTP cable to connect PCs to a hub. The UTP cable has RJ45 connectors at each end and these are wired up according to the TIA/EIA 568 A or TIA/EIA 568 B specification. The four pairs of wires are coloured, one wire being solid colour and the other of the pair being white with a dash of the same colour at short intervals. When looking at the RJ45 plug from the cable end and with the retaining clip downwards the left hand pin is referred to as pin 1 and the right hand pin as pin 8. The colours (for the A version) are white green, green, white orange, blue, white blue, orange, white brown, brown. The colours (for the B version) are white orange, orange, white green, blue, white blue, green, white brown, brown. You will notice that just the orange and green pairs have been interchanged.

CRUCIAL TIP

For connection from a PC to a hub both ends of the cable are wired up in the same way, this is referred to as a 'straight-through cable'. For 10 Mbs only the green and orange pairs are used. In my organisation we use the B version normally for a straight-through cable.

If you just want to connect one PC to another you need to connect the transmit connection of one of the PCs to the receive connection of the other and vice versa. You achieve this by wiring one end according to TIA/EIA 568 A and the other end according to TIA/EIA 568 B. This is referred to as a 'cross-over cable'.

CRUCIAL TIP

There is an indicator light on NICs and hubs (and other network devices). If the light does not come on when a network cable is plugged in there is a fault somewhere. If the light comes on when the cable is plugged in, the system may be working. When you make the last connection in a sequence always check that the light(s) comes on.

Section 5

The OSI and TCP/IP reference models

This section describes ways of dividing up the complex problem of communication into smaller more tractable problems.

CRUCIAL CONCEPT

Communication is a complicated subject and when you have a complicated problem it is usual to break it down into simpler parts. For example – building a house is complicated but we bring in different skills workers who can solve the separate problems. One worker will deal with the brickwork, another the carpentry, another the plumbing, another the electrical installation and many others. The ISO (International Standards Organisation) defined a reference model for data communications – the **OSI (Open System Interconnection) reference model**. This is a seven-layer model dividing up the problem of communication and hopefully making it easier for different manufacturers' equipment to work together.

If you think about sending a get well card to a friend the fundamental aim is to transfer the idea of the message to your friend. There are a number of steps:

A. You write the message on the card.
B. You put the card into the envelope and you address and stamp the envelope.
C. You put the envelope into a letterbox.
D. The postman collects the letters from the letterbox and takes them to the sorting office – there may be other steps here.
E. A sorter sorts the letters.
F. Another postman puts the letter through your friend's letterbox.
G. Your friend takes the letter out of its envelope.
H. Your friend reads the message.

All of the steps from B to G were there to provide the service for steps A and H. Steps C to F were there to deal with the envelope, from it entering the letterbox to it appearing at your friend's letterbox. Steps B and G were necessary, but nothing to do with the meaning of the message, and could equally well have been done by someone else in the houses at each end. As you are studying the OSI model think about the communication described above and you will see many similarities.

The OSI model is based on the idea of separation of responsibility for different phases of the communication. Not strictly part of the OSI model is the movement of the communication from place to place over the physical medium (UTP, STP, optical fibre . . .).

Layer 1.   The **physical layer** is to do with the interface with the physical medium.
Layer 2.   The **data link layer** deals with reliable communication between two devices.
Layer 3.   The **network layer** deals with routing the package from the source machine to the destination machine.
Layer 4.   The **transport layer** deals with the efficient, reliable transport of the whole message from end to end.
Layer 5.   The **session layer** establishes, manages and terminates sessions between applications.
Layer 6.   The **presentation layer** ensures that the data is in the correct form to be understood.
Layer 7.   The **application layer** provides a satisfactory environment for the application programs.

127

The model is normally shown with Layer 7 at the top and Layer 1 at the bottom.

7: Application
6: Presentation
5: Session
4: Transport
3: Network
2: Data Link
1: Physical

The TCP/IP model

Before the OSI model was published the American Department of Defense had a network built between research establishments which were part of DARPA (Defense Advanced Research Projects Agency). This developed into a more extensive network which included non-defense establishments – ARPA (Advanced Research Projects Agency). It spread across the borders of the USA and developed into the first part of the Internet. There was a need to communicate with great reliability (this was in the time of the cold war and the network was designed to withstand a nuclear attack by building in a large amount of redundancy). Two complementary components were created – TCP (Transport Control Protocol) and IP (Internet Protocol). A minimal layered structure was built around them, shown below, TCP providing the main functionality of the OSI transport layer (layer 4) and IP that of the OSI network layer (layer 3), although the division of functions between the two is not the same as in the OSI model. There are several application support packages in common use e.g. FTP (File Transfer Protocol), Telnet (a simple terminal software package), SMTP (Simple Mail Transfer Protocol). TCP/IP does not address the network access function.

Application
Transport – TCP
Network – IP
Network Access

Although it does not conform to the OSI model, TCP/IP is by far the most commonly used 'protocol stack' in modern networking, and is the basis for the Internet. Despite this, from now on the text will refer to the OSI model unless otherwise stated, in line with common practice in the communications industry.

The physical layer (1)

This layer, unlike most, if not all, of the others is normally implemented in hardware. It is built into the NIC. You must purchase the correct NIC for the sort of network it is to connect to: a Token Ring NIC for a Token Ring network, an NIC with RJ45 socket for a UTP Ethernet network (although some Ethernet NICs have several different sockets – AUI (Auxiliary Unit Interface), BNC (British Naval Connector, for thin co-ax)). The physical layer takes bits and places them on the network medium. In the Ethernet case it deals with reporting to the data link layer (usually on the NIC as well) whether there is traffic on the medium, and when it is transmitting it is listening for a collision and if one occurs it reports that to the data link layer which arranges for the data to be retransmitted. The physical layer is also responsible for reception of data from the medium – it is not interested in who originated the data or whether it is destined for this machine or not, it just passes the bits up to the data link layer.

The data link layer (2)

This layer accepts packets from the network layer for transmission to other devices on its immediate network. It **encapsulates** them into one or more frames and when there is silence on the medium and it has waited as appropriate, it delivers them as bits to the physical layer. It also accepts bits from the physical layer, **de-encapsulates** them and delivers the packet to the network layer.

Whatever the LAN technology, if the medium is shared, the destination machine must be able to recognise that the frame is for itself. Therefore there must be some sort of addressing. Each NIC has a number that is unique. The number is 6 bytes long. The first 3 bytes identify the manufacturer and the last 3 are specified by the manufacturer. The 6-byte number is called the MAC (media access control) address of the NIC. Each frame has a header containing the Destination MAC address, the Source MAC address and some other information, and a trailer containing an error detecting checksum. In between is the data which is to be transferred from the network layer on the source side to the network layer on the destination side. These may, or may not, be the machines at the ends of the communication. You could envisage the encapsulation at this level like the bagging and labelling of a bag of mail going from one town to another. The bag will have a label with the destination town on it and possibly also where it came from. The bag and the label are removed (de-encapsulation) at the next town where they may be sorted and some go on to further towns. This is not a perfect analogy as at this layer, and at higher layers, large messages may actually be split up into smaller parts for transmission and, in LANs, are not aggregated with other messages.

The network layer (3)

This layer accepts a segment from the transport layer and, after encapsulating it, sends it either to its destination host, or to another router on the way to its destination. We will spend some more time on this in the next chapter.

The transport layer (4)

This layer accepts an arbitrarily long message from the session layer and, if necessary, divides it up into pieces and delivers it to the network layer for transmission to the destination. It may work in either of two ways – **connection oriented** or **connectionless**. Connection oriented means that a connection is established with the transport layer at the other end of the communication and only then is data transferred (rather like the telephone). When all the data has been transferred the connection is terminated. With connectionless communication each transfer of data is independent of any other (rather like letters). The transport layer does not check on the successful transmission of connectionless segments.

The session layer (5)

Establishes, manages and terminates sessions between two communicating hosts. We will not be discussing this any further.

The presentation layer (6)

Ensures that the receiving application can understand what it is receiving. Some computers encode text in ASCII, others in EBCDIC. If hosts using different encoding are communicating, it is the presentation layer that should do the translation.

The application layer (7)

Provides services to applications that are outside the OSI model.

Section 6

End of chapter assessment

Multiple-choice questions

1. What is the term used to describe the maximum number of bits that can be transmitted in a given amount of time?
   a) conductance
   b) bandwidth
   c) impedance
   d) propagation
   e) latency

2. What factor increases delays on a network?
   a) increased number of users
   b) decreased number of users
   c) increased memory size
   d) increased size of hard drive
   e) decreased size of hard drive

3. Which one of these would not normally be considered to be a 'device' in an operating system?
   a) laser printer
   b) magnetic disk drive
   c) CD-ROM drive
   d) system memory
   e) ethernet adapter

4. What is the function of the session layer?
   a) provides reliable transfer of data across the physical layer
   b) manages and terminates sessions between applications
   c) provides services to the application layer
   d) provides connectivity and path selection between two end systems
   e) none of the above

5. If you wish to create a network of just two PCs, what kind of cable would be used to directly connect them?
   a) a UTP straight through cable
   b) a UTP cross-over cable
   c) a UTP roll-over cable
   d) a multi-mode fibre optic cable
   e) a mono-mode fibre optic cable

6. In electricity what is meant by AC?
   a) attenuated current
   b) amplified current
   c) alternating current
   d) alternative current
   e) amplitude circuit

7. What is the name given to the opposition to the flow of electrons through materials?
   a) ohms
   b) voltage
   c) resistance
   d) current
   e) inductance

8. What is the cause of cross-talk?
   a) electrical motors or lighting
   b) the cable going through a noisy office
   c) arriving at work late
   d) cable wires that are too wide in diameter
   e) electrical noise from other wires in a cable

9. Which term describes the conversion of bits into a form that can travel on a physical communications link?
   a) encoding
   b) decrypting
   c) encrypting
   d) decoding
   e) reforming

10. What does the twisting of the wires do in UTP cable?
    a) makes it bend more easily
    b) makes it less expensive
    c) reduces noise pickup
    d) allows four pairs to fit in the space of two
    e) helps the engineer to fit an RJ45 plug more easily

11. What type of network cable is now installed most often for Ethernet cabling?
    a) 50 ohm co-axial cable
    b) 75 ohm co-axial cable
    c) 150 ohm shielded twisted pair cable
    d) 100 ohm unshielded twisted pair cable
    e) 62.5/125 multi-mode fibre optic cable

Multiple-choice answers

1-b, 2-a, 3-d, 4-b, 5-b, 6-c, 7-c, 8-e, 9-a, 10-c, 11-d.

Chapter 12
Addressing and routing

Chapter summary

The data link layer and the network layer need to deliver the data sent by the layers above to their proper destinations. The two layers use different means of addressing that solve their different problems. This chapter gives a short but concentrated account.

Learning outcomes

After studying this chapter you should aim to test your achievement by answering the multiple-choice questions and the examples at the end of the chapter. You should be able to do the following things.

Outcome 1: Explain the concept and purpose of protocols.
Outcome 2: Explain the structure and purpose of a 'layer 2' address, identify layer 2 devices explain the effects of layer 2 devices on data flow and how a host determines the layer 2 address of another host.
Outcome 3: Explain the structure and purpose of a 'layer 3' address, distinguish between the different classes of IP address and explain the concept and purpose of subnetting.

How will you be assessed on this?

Assessment of this is probably on the basis of facts, which may well be assessed using multiple-choice questions.

Useful information sources

Cisco Systems http://www.cisco.com
Routing and the Network Layer http://www.cs.rpi.edu/courses/netprog/lectures/ppthtml/routing/
Routers http://www.rad.com/networks/1997/nettut/router.html
IP Addressing Architecture http://www.rad.com/networks/1994/ip_addr/tcpip2.htm

Section 1

Network addresses and protocols

This section introduces the concepts of network address space and protocols and looks at the relationship between the two. The common data link layer protocols are explained.

The data link layer addresses

On any system in which many computers are connected to a shared communications medium there is a need to identify where a message is intended to go. Every network must have its own address space of addresses, and some have several, overlaid on each other. In

Ethernet networks the address space is worldwide. Every NIC (network interface card) has its unique address permanently stored on the card – the MAC address (media access control address). It is a 48-bit number, usually displayed in hexadecimal (about 256,000,000,000,000 different numbers). The first 3 bytes, the 'organisational unique identifier' indicate the manufacturer. The next 3 bytes, the 'vendor assigned number', are unique for that manufacture.

Example: Cisco has been allocated an OUI of 00 60 2F and has chosen 3B 45 8D for the VAN for one of the interfaces of a switch so the MAC address is 00 60 2F 3B 45 8D.

Other network technologies have name spaces which are confined to one network. When these are connected together into an internetwork a 'bridge' is required between the two networks.

C R U C I A L   C O N C E P T

Protocol is the set of rules for the structure of messages. It is essential, for communication to happen, that the receiving device knows what information is being passed by which bits or bytes.

The data link layer protocols

Each LAN type has its own protocol, suited to its topology and the purposes it was originally designed for.

Token Ring protocol

The structure of a Token Ring frame is:

Bytes	1	1	1	6	6	⩾0	4	4	4
	Start delimiter	Access control	Frame control	Destination address	Source address	Data	F C S	End delimiter	Frame status

The meaning of the fields is as follows.

- Start delimiter. A 'wake up' byte.
- Access control. A byte to specify priority and reservation and a token or monitor bit. If the token bit is set this is the token and only the 'end delimiter' byte follows.
- Frame control. This indicates whether this frame contains data or is a control frame, and if it is control what type it is.
- Destination address. The MAC address of the destination host.
- Source address. The MAC address of the sender.
- Data. The information to be sent if this is not a control frame.
- FCS. Frame check sequence – A 4-byte CRC (cyclic redundancy check) calculated from the frame contents. The receiving host recalculates this and if the result matches the likelihood of corruption is very small.
- End delimiter. Defines the end of the frame.
- Frame status. A field which can be modified by the destination host to indicate that the frame was received.

Token Ring uses differential Manchester encoding. This is a serial encoding scheme in which the signal changes state at the beginning of each 'bit cell' to denote a '0' and both at the beginning and in the middle of the cell to denote a '1'. It is shown below. This allows easy extraction of the clock and signal from the bit stream.

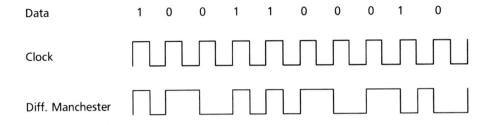

The FDDI protocol

FDDI stands for fiber distributed data Interface, it is a faster (100 Mbps) variety of Token Ring, using a double ring topology using fibre optic media (although 'copper' variants do exist). The structure of an FDDI frame is the same as IBM's Token Ring with the addition of a preamble before the start delimiter. The encoding system is more efficient, using 4B/5B (4 bits is encoded in 5 bits – Manchester is 1B/2B).

Ethernet

The term Ethernet is commonly used to describe the original network designed by Xerox in the early 1970s, the basis for the IEEE 802.3 standard released in 1980. Ethernet provides services at both layer 1 and layer 2 of the OSI reference model, but does not define a logical link control (LLC) protocol. These parts are implemented in hardware, usually on a card in a host computer or on the motherboard of the host computer.

The structure of an Ethernet (IEEE 802.3) frame is:

Bytes	7	1	6	6	2	64 - 1500	4
	Preamble	Start delimiter	Destination address	Source address	Length	802.2 header and data	FCS

The meaning of the fields is as follows:

- Preamble is an alternating pattern of ones and zeros allowing the receiving host to synchronise with the sender's clock.
- Start delimiter is 10101011, where this continues the pattern of the preamble with the exception of the two 1s at the end.
- Source address is the address of the host that sent the frame.
- Destination address may be that of one host, or could be the address of a group or the 'broadcast address' of all ones.
- Type (Ethernet) specifies the upper layer protocol to receive the data.
- Length (IEEE 802.3) indicates the number of bytes in the data field. To guarantee the detection of collisions the minimum is 64.
- Data in the frame is sent to an upper layer protocol which is specified in the type field (Ethernet) or in the data field (802.3).
- FCS – the frame check sequence is a 4-byte CRC.

IEEE 802.3 specifies the physical layer requirements for a number of different media. These are referred to in a form of the type <bitrate in Mbit/s> <modulation method> <physical medium code>, such as 10BASE5, as described in the last chapter. The most common is 10BASET, which is 10 Mbps, Baseband on UTP. Cat 5e (enhanced category 5) is only a little more expensive than the commonly used Cat 3 and allows for upgrading without cable reinstallation. Transmission is on one twisted wire pair while reception occurs on another pair (the other two pairs are not used at this speed). Manchester encoding is used.

Section 2

Connecting networks

This section describes how networks are connected together using repeaters and hubs, explains the difference between the two and explains when one or the other might be required.

Repeaters and hubs

With 10BASE2 (thin co-ax) hosts are attached directly to the cable with a tee piece. (This is a 'passive' network, there are no electronics in the backbone of the network). If a distance of greater than 200 m is required a repeater is needed.

> ───────────── CRUCIAL CONCEPT ─────────────
>
> The **repeater** receives the degraded signal and resends it having amplified and retimed it. No understanding of the frame structure occurs. The repeater is a layer 1 device.

With 10BASET each cable goes from one piece of electronics to one other, it is an 'active' network. Connecting to a group of other hosts is achieved by a 'hub', or multi-port repeater which sends out any signal it receives to every other port. The maximum length of a cable is 100 m. Hubs may be attached to other hubs or repeaters, to add extra connections or extend length, up to four between any two hosts.

The TIA/EIA 568 A standard specifies a maximum of 90 m for the horizontal cabling, a patch cord of 3 m between the host and the telecom socket and a 6 m patch cord at the horizontal cross connect. (Cabling from the wiring closet or hub to the hosts is called horizontal cabling, while cabling between wiring closets, or between buildings that are part of the same LAN, is called vertical cabling or backbone cabling.)

The network interface card carries out both layer 1 and layer 2 functions. It encapsulates the data into frame(s) (layer 2), provides structured access to the shared access media and sends the frame out on the media (layer 1).

Access control in Ethernet: CSMA/CD

All the hosts attached receive all frames, since the repeaters simply retransmit everything sent to them. The access control mechanism is distributed using the CSMA/CD protocol. If a host with data to send detects no signal on the medium it will start transmitting. Another host may also have started transmitting but their signals have not yet reached the other host. When they do each host detects the 'collision'. The medium that is subject to the possibility of a collision is called the collision domain. The larger it is, the more likely are collisions, which reduce the useful performance of the network.

Bridges and switches

For this reason, as the number of hosts increases the overall traffic on the network increases and the 'effective bandwidth' decreases, to a point where there may not be enough to carry all the traffic. To overcome this problem it is possible to split it into two or more segments using a 'bridge'.

> ───────────── CRUCIAL CONCEPT ─────────────
>
> A **bridge** is like an intelligent repeater between the segments. It receives a frame and notes the MAC address of the destination and if this is on the other segment, or it does not know the address, it forwards the frame on the other segment.

The bridge also notes the source address and which side of the bridge it arrived from so that in future it will know where that host is. Frames for destinations in the same segment as the source do not leave their own segment. The effect is to reduce the size of the collision domain (by increasing the number of them). A bridge may provide the link between segments with different layer 2 protocols.

---CRUCIAL CONCEPT---

A switch is a multi-port bridge.

These are layer 2 devices (with built in layer 1 hardware). There is an increase in latency caused by a bridge as the whole frame is received before being sent on its way. It may be reduced by a process called 'cut through' where the frame is read only as far as the destination address before the decision is made whether to transmit it or not. Advanced switches allow more than one message to travel through the switch at once and, if the NICs attached are capable of it, they may be set to full duplex communication, i.e. data flowing in both directions at once.

Section 3

Network layer addressing

This section describes the network layer addressing system, usually provided as part of the Internet protocol (IP).

Why another layer of addresses is needed

There is no information in the MAC address that indicates where a host is located. In order to deliver a message to a host at some particular location another method must be used. IP addresses attempt to deal with this problem.

IP addresses

IP addresses are 4 bytes (32 bits) in length. In an attempt to make them 'user friendly' they are normally stated as four denary numbers with a full stop between them – 'dotted denary', for example 170.241.56.12. The first part is the network number and the last part is the host number within that network.

IP addresses and IP protocol at version 4 has been in use for about 30 years when there were many fewer networks (we will shortly be moving to IP Version 6). The addresses are divided between three major classes of network, defined as follows.

- Class A: a small number (126) of very large networks;
- Class B: a moderate number (~16,000) of large networks;
- Class C: a large number (~2,000,000) of small networks.

Network IP addresses are allocated by the American Registry for Internet Numbers (ARIN). (After all the Internet is a development of the American ARPANET.)

Class A networks

These are allocated to governments and very large organisations. The first byte has a zero in the leftmost bit so the number here may be from 1 to 126. (127 is reserved for a special purpose.) The remaining 3 bytes may be used for the hosts. (A host number of all zeros or all ones is not allowed.) The host address range can use the remaining 3 bytes.

Class B networks

The leftmost 2 bits are 10. The remaining 6 bits of the first byte and the whole of the second byte are used to specify the network (addresses from 128.0.0.0 to 191.255.0.0). The host address range can use the remaining 2 bytes.

Class C networks

The leftmost 3 bits are 110. The remaining 5 bits of the first byte and the whole of bytes 2 and 3 are used to specify the network (addresses from 192.0.0.0 to 223.255.255.0). Byte 4 specifies the hosts. Addresses from 224 upwards (with an initial three ones) are reserved for other purposes.

There is one Class A network defined for private use (they must not be connected to the Internet). It is 10.0.0.0. Also a Class B network, 172.16.0.0. And 255 Class C networks – 192.168.0.0 to 192.168.255.0.

In order to find the IP address of a company there is a hierarchical series of Domain Name Servers which will translate a domain name such as 'www.cisco.com' into its IP address.

Subnetting

With a Class A address three of the bytes of the IP address are for hosts. This amounts to 24 bits or around 16 million hosts, too much for a single directly connected network. To divide up the network into manageable segments, some of the (least significant) bits of the address are defined to be the host part and the rest as the network and sub-network part by means of a sub-net mask in which ones correspond to the part of the address which is the network and sub-network while the zeros correspond to the host portion of the address, usually presented as dotted denary. If we have a Class A address 10.0.0.0 and a subnet mask of 255.255.0.0 the network portion is the first 8 bits, the subnet corresponds to the second 255, leaving 16 bits for the host part, giving a total of 256 subnets each with 65536 hosts. The host address 0 is not allowed as this is used to describe, or address, the network itself and the host address 65535 (all ones) is used as the broadcast address, reducing the number by two. The same rule applies to subnets, so in this case there could only actually be 254 subnets.

Example
We have a Class C network 192.168.200.0 and need to split it up into six subnets. The total number of sub-nets is two more than this so eight subnets total is required, and this requires 3 bits. So the subnet mask needed (in binary) is 11111111.11111111.11111111.11100000 leaving 5 bits for the hosts, i.e. 32 total or 30 useable. The first of the subnets is 192.168.200.32 and the first host in that network is 192.168.200.33.

CRUCIAL CONCEPT

A **router** is like a switch but operates at the network layer and can switch messages between networks.

Address resolution protocol

When a router or host, A, on an Ethernet network sends a message to another device, B, whose IP address it knows, it has to address the other device by use of its MAC address. If A has not been switched on for long or B has not been involved in any communication A may not know B's address. A issues an ARP request (a broadcast asking 'Anyone know this IP address?'). B responds with an acknowledgement frame with its MAC address in the header, which A stores along with the IP address in its 'ARP cache', then sends the message to its destination. If the destination machine is not on the same network but a router knows where it is, it will give its own MAC address so that any messages will be sent to the router which will forward it.

Section 4

End of chapter assessment

Multiple-choice questions

1. If three hosts are connected to a hub, how many IP addresses are required by these four devices?
   a) one
   b) two
   c) three
   d) four
   e) five

2. What correctly describes a source address?
   a) information that is transmitted from machine to machine
   b) the address of a machine that receives data from another machine in the network
   c) the address of a machine that sends data to and information to other machines in a network
   d) the MAC address of a switch
   e) The IP address of a hub

3. Which of the following best describes networking protocols?
   a) the use of the same manufacturer's hardware throughout a network
   b) a set of utilities that can be used by a network manager
   c) the layers of the OSI model
   d) a set of rules that describe how devices should exchange information
   e) both a and c above

4. Which statement best describes bridges?
   a) they operate at OSI layer 2 and use MAC addresses to make decisions
   b) they operate at OSI layer 2 and use IP addresses to make decisions
   c) they operate at OSI layer 3 and use MAC addresses to make decisions
   d) they operate at OSI layer 3 and use IP addresses to make decisions
   e) they provide a secret way for network engineers to get between buildings

5. What is another name for a multi-port repeater?
   a) a bridge
   b) a hub
   c) a router
   d) a host
   e) a gateway

6. At which layer of the OSI model is the NIC located?
   a) layer 1
   b) layer 2
   c) layer 3
   d) both 1 and 2
   e) both 2 and 3

7. What is a characteristic of a collision domain?
   a) all computers in a switch connected LAN
   b) all computers in a WAN
   c) all computers on a single shared access medium
   d) all computer sharing a single IP address
   e) all computers sharing a single MAC address

8. What is the term used for separating collision domains with bridges, switches and routers?
    a) switching domains
    b) fragmentation
    c) segmentation
    d) extending domains
    e) separation

9. What is the organisational unique identifier (OUI)?
    a) the first 6 bytes of the MAC address
    b) the first 6 hex digits of the MAC address
    c) the first 6 bits of the MAC address
    d) all of the hex digits of the MAC address
    e) the last 6 hex digits of the MAC address

10. What device can help solve the problem of too much traffic on a network by dividing the network into segments and filtering traffic based on the MAC address?
    a) repeater
    b) hub
    c) bridge
    d) router
    e) gateway

11. Which of the following are true of routers?
    a) they base forwarding decisions on the basis of network layer addresses
    b) they base forwarding decisions on the basis of MAC addresses
    c) they operate only at the data link layer
    d) they operate at the data link and physical layer
    e) they always have exactly two ports

12. Which of the following is the approximate number of hosts in a Class B unsubnetted network?
    a) 254
    b) 2040
    c) 16,400
    d) 65,500
    e) 16 million

13. How many bits must be borrowed from the host portion of a Class B address if we require 500 subnets?
    a) 6
    b) 7
    c) 8
    d) 9
    e) 10

14. When sending data to a host on a different network, the source host encapsulates data so that it contains what destination address in the IP header?
    a) the IP address of the router
    b) the IP address of the destination host
    c) the MAC address of the router
    d) the MAC address of the destination host
    e) the TCP address of the destination host

15. What protocol will find the MAC address of a device given its IP address?
    a) RARP
    b) proxy RARP
    c) DNS
    d) DHCP
    e) ARP

Multiple-choice answers

1-c, 2-c, 3-d, 4-a, 5-b, 6-d, 7-c, 8-c, 9-b, 10-c, 11-a, 12-d, 13-d, 14-b, 15-e.

Index

abacus, 5
abstraction layers, 89
adder, 25-27, 39
address, 42, 91, 132, 136
address resolution protocol, 137
ALU (arithmetic and logic unit), 39-47, 61
API (applications programming interface),
   89-90, 95, 100, 102-105, 113
Apple Macintosh, 88
application software, 10
argument string, 112
arithmetic circuits, 25
artificial intelligence, 6
assembly language, 6
attenuation, 121
auxiliary memory, 51, 53
auxiliary storage devices, 54-56

Babbage, Charles, 5
backing store, 92
bandwidth, 51, 66-67
binary number system, 14-16, 23, 27, 44
BIOS (basic input output system), 54
bit, 14-17, 22-24, 32, 45, 72
block devices, 71
blocks, 93
Boolean algebra, 17-21, 26
  associative laws, 19
  communicative laws, 19
  de Morgan's law, 20
  distributive laws, 20
Brahe, Tyche, 4
bridge, 135-136
broadband, 76
buses, 8-10, 25, 38, 42-43, 45, 47, 60, 71,
  83, 124-125
byte, 15, 51, 93

C, 39, 64
cache, 52-53, 60, 66-67, 80
canonical form, 20-21
card readers, 77
CD-ROM, 8, 45, 56
central memory, 51
character device, 71
chip, 6, 38, 81
circuit synthesis, 20-21
circuits, 120-123

CISC (complex instruction set computers),
  63-64
class A networks, 136
class B networks, 137
class C networks, 137
CLI (command line interpreter), 110-113
clock rate, 60-61
COBOL (common business orientated
  language), 6
COLOSSUS, 5
combinatorial circuits, 20, 21-28, 33
command dialogue, 111
command line user interfaces, 111-112
compiler, 64-65
computers
  definition, 5
  generations, 5-7
  historical development, 5-7
  inventors, 5
control unit, 41
CPI (clocks per second), 61-62
CPU (central processing unit), 7-10, 38-42,
  45, 51-53, 94
cross-talk, 122
CRT (cathode ray tube), 74
CSMA/CD, 135

D-type latch, 31
data, 4-5, 16, 38, 52-53, 60, 93
data link layer addresses, 132-133
data link layer protocols, 133
DBMS (database management system), 9
decoders, 22-23
demultiplexer, 25
device driver, 95
device independence, 95
device management, 94-95
digital camera, 7
digital circuits, 18
disk, 8, 10, 45, 53, 55-56, 80
displays, 74-75
display resolution, 74
DMA device, 72
DMUX (demultiplexer), 25
drives, 8
DVD, 56

encoders, 23-25

Printed in the United Kingdom
by Lightning Source UK Ltd.
134176UK00001B/47/P